Is Christian Life Possible Today?

by

Karl Rahner

Dimension Books ● **Denville, New Jersey**

First English Edition Published by Dimension Books, Inc. P.O. Box 811, Denville, N.J. 07834. The work is a translation of *Mein Problem: Karl Rahner Antwortet Jungen Menschen,* originally published by Verlag Herder, Freiburg in Breisgau. The translation was made by Salvator Attanasio. Copyright • 1984 this edition by Dimension Books, Inc.

ISBN 0-87193-210-5

TABLE OF CONTENTS

PREFACE

This book came into being thanks to a priest active in the pastoral care of young people in a big city who suggested that people write letters to me about their problems in leading a Christian life. Perhaps he praised me unduly to these people and held out to them expectations quite beyond my capacity to fulfill. Then, gently but firmly, he persuaded me to answer their letters or at least make an attempt at doing so.

Hence these letters are authentic. What these young people write about covers problems of real life that particularly concern and affect them. They are reproduced here undoctored, though slight omissions occur here and there only where discretion dictated shielding the correspondent's identity. The names in the salutation were also changed for the same reason.*

I believe that the letters as such, independent of my replies, are significant. They enable other young people, as well as pastors, parents and teachers, to gain an insight into what is going on in the minds of today's young generation. Hence one should not only reflect on what I have written in reply, but also try to learn something from the letters themselves. These letters, manifestly, were composed within the compass of a particular, limited, socio-economic milieu.

---

*The Publisher of this edition has taken the liberty of substituting names more commonly used in the anglo-saxon world so as not to distract the reader.

Clearly their authors are not young people who are starving, nor are they among those entangled in the drug scene. They were written by normal human beings whose problems merit serious attention just as much as those that trouble people in extreme life-situations.

My answers to these letters make no claim to any complete mastery of the problem-complex articulated in them. Young people generally pose questions that reveal the totality of the life that they happen to be leading at a particular age. Such questions can never be fully and wholly answered. Accordingly what is stated here, measured against the questions themselves, is limited and incomplete.

Nor am I really certain that my replies have done justice, even approximately, to the mentality of these young people. I tried to answer their letters as a Christian. But in the letters themselves and, more than ever, in my answers, the ultimate depth of Christianity's message is not really touched upon. Of this I am altogether aware. The letters revolve, not wholly but mostly, around human affairs and problems which lie only on the perimeter of the quintessential reality that Christianity proclaims in the revelation of the living God in Jesus. Nevertheless I felt that one should also discuss such themes with young persons without, however, intending to produce the impression that a horizontal, one-dimensional humanism is all that we have to offer to young people today.

I have gladly answered these letters even when they seemed to lie outside the radius of my normal vocational tasks and, in so doing, I learned something from them. Perhaps the reader of these letters can also perceive that and here and there he or she can learn something from my brief answers to them.

Karl Rahner

ONE

WHERE IS HAPPINESS FOR A HUMAN BEING?

Dear Father Rahner,

I would like to write you something on happiness and being happy. But I am probably the wrong person to say something on this precise subject. You will see for yourself.

I live in comfortable bourgeois circumstances. I have brothers and sisters and non-separated parents, owners of a house and a car. We are in short, viewed from without, the "good and happy family." In this family which has been distinguished through the accomplishments of five persons, one member has become a black sheep. He pursues other aims, adopts a life-style that unfolds at night, he drinks, smokes, once changed schools and now has even been expelled from the school of his choice. So that you don't have to guess! I am this person.

My father and mother have worriedly made plans for me which I will list in proper order: send him off to a school that will reform him? No, better not, a detailed list of strict 'do's and don't's' might be better. Get him out of the house and order him to live in an entirely different neighborhood far from us? No, better not that either. Might more 'do's and don't's' be better? This edifying cycle of failed plans for me has been repeated frequently within a two-year period.

In school this "nobody"—the nickname that's been pinned on me everywhere—was a first rate pupil up to the ninth grade. Then his marks suddenly began to drop, his dress to become sloppier, his hair wilder. "A typical sign of decline," people always say. Two years later this "nobody" changed schools but only for a year after which he again was kicked out, this time for good. In the principal's report the reason for the expulsion was attributed to "statements inappropriate in the school setting" and to "standing senselessly on the window sill."

Now this "nobody" is out of school, has nothing to do and writes a letter to Karl Rahner on happiness. Happiness is that magic state that we seek, that we venerate and covet. The very word causes more people to die rather than to enter into life. My friends are also looking for happiness. "Friends" is hardly the right word here. If I'm ever in need, none of them will help me because none can help. For they themselves are too deeply stuck in this "happy" world. Or at least they continue to pursue the myth of happiness. They hang around, smoke pot or sniff heroin (sometimes they also cut "snow" but the stuff is hard to come by here)—and they wait. "Things go best with me when I can't think," says one of them. But he hasn't found his happiness, he merely slows down his meaningless life.

Another one signs in at the hospital at least every two weeks where they pump out his stomach, strengthen his blood and release him again. They know he'll show up again and he always laughs when

he does come back. "Here I am again," he announces, often with the brief, ritual, postscriptural
"one more time" which sounds like an expression of
astonishment. He laughs, but he has not found his
happiness.

Then one looks them in the face. An eye to eye
encounter takes place. They are then quite simple to
understand, these assertedly stranded souls whose only mistake was no longer to cling to their self-
awareness. And whose death sentence is to understand that for them, and for me, for an all too long
time there has been no chance to follow any other
course—any wholly other course.

Happiness, being-happy—a devilish magnet that
draws you and spins you around, that destroys you
through its awesome might.

I like my crowd because they talk without thinking what happiness could mean. They react simply
and spontaneously because they've thrown in the
towel. They are done with their search, not because
they have arrived at a solution but because they can
no longer endure it. They are aware of this and they
live with this awareness, self-destructively, pursuing
the great goal—happiness.

Happiness makes me want to reach out for
flight, just as they do—flight from myself because my
old milieu is now far off, it exists no more. I broke
away from home at the age of 15 and have entered into a series of relationships with all my feelings. I have
escaped into love and I have exploited it in order to be
weak, without myself noticing it. I have plunged into
religion in order to try to realize perhaps that it is
something I don't want. I have plunged into alcohol
in order to weep without being ashamed of myself.
And I have plunged into drugs in order to be able to

live without having to think, and I have again extricated myself from them in order to be able to seek further.

Dear Father Rahner, from all this I have but one question: do you know an answer? Where is happiness for a human being?

Norbert

Dear Norbert,

What astonishes me most in your letter at first sight, aside from my consternation, is the honesty, indeed the hardness of your self-portrait. What haven't you not suffered in your 17 years! I might be tempted to praise you, especially for your bitter, self-critical honesty. But then I stop myself short again and I ask myself: what really lies hidden there? How can one treat oneself so, seize oneself (so to speak) by the scruff of the neck and jolt oneself, indeed almost revile oneself: Is it once again just a trick, another way to reach out for a portion of that happiness which you are longing for and which you refuse to give up?

You know, of course, that I am not a depth psychologist, nor even an ordinary psychologist. Therefore I would like simply to pose this question to you without being able to answer it. When you revile yourself so much and actually praise the other members of your family, expressly or secretly, obviously it is because somewhere you recognize a standard, a goal that you wish were really right for you and in terms of which you could then judge yourself.

Why don't you therefore admit more directly, and also more courageously, that in the final analysis you want to be something other than what you are, you want to be able to live differently than the way you are living now? That you are not really trying to overcome this disharmony you experience and that, instead, you persevere in your life-style with a remarkable obstinacy and—just admit it!—almost proudly so and that somehow you exult in your present way of life? Is this the real reason why you can do nothing else but live as you are actually living now? And why, almost like a man who would gladly like to walk but who limps because of a fractured leg, you can't do anything about it and as a result are basically not to blame for anything?

I don't want to believe that and hope that the situation is otherwise.

Or—I continue my question—are things such in your mind that to you the happiness of a more "normal" life (to which you would to some extent like to comply and satisfy the demands that you yourself make on yourself) would appear to you in reality to be so petty and paltry that you cannot see why one ought to live so "normally" and "reasonably." Is the tiny bit of happiness that might come from a more "normal" life-style, that of your parents and brothers and sisters, really nothing in the depths of your mind? Is it no more than the disappointing "happiness" that you are now depriving your life of, even when you are not able to renounce it despite your disappointment with it?

I don't know whether by posing this question I have really touched upon your real life-problem. But I'll try once more. Let me put it this way: you demand too much happiness. What you are demanding, you will not find in a normal bourgeois life. So you look for it in another way and as a result you are disappointed. How would it be if you were to give up this exaggerated demand for happiness? And, of course, you will immediately say: why should I give it up? Who forces me, you can also say, not to demand so much from life?

I believe that behind such an exaggerated demand for happiness there lurks a secret, very effectively disguised unbelief in it, even though you are not conscious of it. You say that you believe in God. But do you really? If God is really the last and ineffable, all-fulfilling happiness toward which one, forgetful of self, ought to strain during one's journey along life's road in order to arrive at true happiness—why do you want to squeeze it here and now into the puny moment in which you are living today? Why can't you wait until it comes as the consummation of life, at the moment of death? Why can't you soberly take upon yourself the commonplace duty, the service of others even though you can't get "high" on it as you can with drugs or other things through which you try to force yourself into a trance of happiness under the name of love, of power or of success?

Why do you want to demand from your life now that it be either a radiant, transporting brightness or a total darkness, period. When you look at your parents and your brothers and sisters you probably tell yourself that after all they are just pitiful, dreary petty-bourgeois people who make the most moderate demands on life and who for that very reason are content when the house is warm and the meals in some measure tolerable, when the earnings are a little higher than the neighbor's, and when the bedroom slippers feel warm and cozy. But it is possible to see all this in another light. Isn't it really impossible to determine once and for all whether this or that interpretation of your family is the right one? For the right interpretation becomes knowable only when the whole of a person's life is viewed retrospectively at the moment of his or her death.

Could not the state of affairs actually be such that your family which appears to you as rather petty-bourgeois and conventional, should really be numbered among those who do not demand great happiness of life instantly and all at once but who instead share the patience, sobriety and courage of those who resolutely struggle along a dusty road day after day? Individuals, accordingly, who make no great demands but patiently await the real, all encompassing happiness that lies in the future? Individuals who courageously can forego trifling experiences of happiness here and now because they are not driven to despair by so-called frustrations, nor do they panic from illusions that they must force happiness into being here and now and specifically through such excesses which you think you must indulge in for the sake of happiness?

What I am saying here seems to be very abstract and sounds like a sermon of the shopworn and dispassionate kind that pastors deliver from the pulpit. But perhaps I am right after all. I don't exactly know how one can bring an individual out of such an inverted fundamental situation as you appear to be in. In old fashioned terms we used to say that this would be possible only through the grace of God. That also happens to be true, but perhaps you can ask yourself whether grace is not being offered to you. Ask yourself whether that which could be called conversion and a total change of life is really so difficult. When you begin, here and now, to do on the very first day of the new life what you in secret perceive as your real duty, namely acceptance of the sober, the bitter, the daily grind, when you will have mustered up the courage to accept the seeming philistinism and boredom of such a duty as the proper one that you are required to do and the one that is slowly moving toward real happiness—when you will have admitted to yourself that you fundamentally have already perceived that your present life-style is no longer the right one and that your reluctance to admit it and your stubborness in pursuing it nevertheless do not signify greatness and courage but a last-ditch cowardice, and when you soberly begin to live normally, without expecting instant sensations of happiness—then the beginning of that conversion for which you yearn, which will still be unaccompanied by any spectacular experience, is already at hand.

You ask me, where is happiness?

I could answer: I don't know. I could say: for me God is the Incomprehensible, the Mystery, period. And I could confess that this God alone can be the all-encompassing and eternal happiness for me. How should I know, therefore, what my happiness looks like concretely? No, I have not yet attained it, but I have an ineffably mysterious presentiment of it and therefore I have no need to deify or idolize the trifling states of happiness of this life. I can simply disregard them and forego them.

The performance of my duties which the petty bourgeois with seeming narrow-mindedness demand of me—a demand which strange to say they are rightfully entitled to make—is nothing else but the courage to go beyond the idols of a bogus happiness of the moment. To go forward toward that happiness that alone deserves the name.

Cordial greetings.

Karl Rahner

TWO

SOMETIMES EVERYTHING BOTHERS ME!

Dear Father Rahner,

Recently I went through a period of deep self-discontent and discovered myself to be incapable of going along on my own way independently of others' help. An outsider would say of me that in such situations in which I am profoundly troubled, in times of disappointment, for example, I lapse into a state of insecurity, even more into one of depression. And my reaction makes it even more difficult to solve my problem: I withdraw into myself and I get mad at everybody.

Concretely: I am assailed by doubts whenever I make a decision independently of my parents, perhaps even against what I think they want. I must add here that I will soon be nineteen, that I greatly respect my parents, but that I am still "in search of my identity." At home I break into tears because I can't and won't put up with certain situations nor even with myself and my own behavior. Then I begin to get annoyed over everything, even over my own tears, and I feel that I am not being taken seriously by those around me and, as I have already said, I withdraw into myself. "She's in a bad mood," "she's quiet and unapproachable" . . . such are the reactions. Often the reverse situation obtains: I behave as if I were in good spirits, approachable, open and friendly to everybody.

Is a mask, a set smile better for someone who suffers such mood swings?

Is an outwardly apparent self-reliance and self-confirmation necessary for me to cope successfully with my discontent? Can I somehow acquire a certain security in order, for example, to be able to react calmly to events, to be in tune with my reactions and even my aggressiveness?

I destroy much of my life, of my joy in life and of my hope as a result of my bad moods. This is surely a matter of impatience with myself ("something has to change"). The upshot of everything is that I often shunt everything off to one side and seclude myself from the outside world.

Perhaps the fault also lies in the fact that I consciously (or unconsciously) would like to get away from my family and have not yet found the right friends—friends who would "accept" me even in such situations. But then, in the larger group, when I must put on something of an act, everything proves unavailing all over again.

That I have come to such a pass, that the problem (these interconnected problems!) that has burdened me for years and from which I feel the constant fear of new days of depression, leaves me with a feeling of hopelessness.

I hope that you will excuse me for this badly composed letter. I have tried to write honestly but I am not happy with the result. It is difficult to write of what is really so deep—and if I did, it would indeed be all too much.

With cordial greetings.

Marie

Dear Marie,

I would probably have to know much more about you in order to be able to give a meaningful answer to your letter. You are still in search, as you say, of your identity. I must honestly confess that I don't know exactly what that means because one, after all, never really knows oneself until the end of his or her life and the so-called identity with oneself is really found when one trustingly delivers oneself, with all his or her contradictions, to God who as scripture says knows our hearts. Indeed he alone knows our hearts.

You speak of your self-contradiction about which you are unhappy. You weep and get annoyed with your own tears. You want to be recognized so you play parts and, at the same time, you consequently revert to bad moods. You wear a mask, as you say, and that does not suit you either; you are seeking autonomy, self-reliance and want it conferred by others. You want to get away from your family and don't truly know just where the circle of friends with whom you would feel accepted is to be found. Every day you are accompanied by the fear of a new bout of depression.

What can one say to all that? Formerly in spiritual literature such a state of feeling was called disconsolation. An attempt was made to set up rules by means of which one could cope with it. Perhaps such rules appear outmoded now and perhaps they lay too much stress on will-power, as they purposed to create the prerequisites through which one can easily jump out of one's skin on command, become another person, a cheerful and amiable being who has bid farewell to disconsolation. But perhaps such rules are not as silly as they sound at first. One should not be annoyed upon being reminded of them but, instead, try patiently and persistently to apply them and test whether they may not be quite sensible and relevant. In St. James it is written: "If anyone of you is in trouble, he should pray." Have you even once tried it? Have you even once brought your feelings of depression to God? Have you ever tried once to trustfully converse with him, even when it may seem to you that you are talking to a blank, dark wall?

In Ignatius of Loyola it is recommended that during such moments of the "darkening of the soul," of anxiety arising from the most varied temptations that drive one to unbelief, to hopelessness, and to lovelessness, one should allow for no changes to take place in one's way of life, in the life-norms that one has given to oneself. One should stick to the decisions that had been taken earlier in calmer and more cheerful states of mind. Indeed, Ignatius even recommends that the good resolutions made in happier times be carried out even more intensively, precisely in times of despair (as he calls it). He says: "Whoever is in despair should make an effort, patiently, to persevere and to reflect that he will soon be consoled, if he most assiduously braces himself against despair."

In trying to interpret feelings of disconsolation, Ignatius points out that they can be the consequence of the fact that, when everything was going rather well with us inwardly and we could have lived happily in respect to religious and human matters, we let ourselves go. It could also be that such a time presents an opportunity for testing our fidelity and steadfastness. And it could also be that in this particular time we should learn that we are weak and really need God's grace and help.

Rules for coping with disconsolation as are found in the spiritual directors of an earlier time can evoke a cynical laugh or bitterness and instant rejection, merely on hearing them. We can think that it was easy for these old gentlemen to talk with their simplistic doctrine and blithely to recommend the exercise of will-power. The frame of mind and interior mood for which they dream up such simple rules is precisely of such a nature that we cannot pray, that we are helplessly delivered to bouts of depression. But if we self-critically examine ourselves, even in such times we will be able to note that we of course cannot do everything, but that we certainly can do something, that there are still different ways of exercising our freedom and responsibility, of comporting ourselves so that we do not simply give up and make depression a cheap or convenient excuse to do nothing.

One possible method, perhaps a very modest one but one which is nevertheless really and readily available, for swimming against the current of depression, is prayer. We can always pray a little. There are also possible methods of more profane character which can be utilized to defend oneself against depression. Why shouldn't one think of others, of how perhaps we can help them, do them a kindness? Why shouldn't we be able to think of a pleasant attentiveness to others? Why couldn't we at least go outdoors and take a walk, instead of sitting and moping around the house? Why couldn't we at least try to discover small useful tricks which make it possible for us to help ourselves? And why shouldn't we also be able to understand and accept these times of depression as a period in the flow of time that will not last forever, as we know very well? Why shouldn't we sternly resolve not to let those around us suffer from our moods, sparing them the fallout?

I know very many cases where persons in such periods of depression clearly knew that it was only a question of once again holding out, of standing their ground through this phase, buttressed by the sober hope that it would and could not last eternally and that one would once again come out of such tunnels that signal various stages of our life's journey. And in certain cases people can hold out in these phases for a rather long time. The person who refuses simply to yield to bouts of depressions and who, once again, tries to skillfully and courageously domesticate them, the person who begins to incorporate them into the great plan of life, such a person will cope with depressions in a good human and Christian way.

But I repeat: in order to give you good advice one should know just where the concrete cause of your bouts of depression lies or at least try to determine their source. You yourself should try to find that out in a better and clearer way. In such matters we can simultaneously be both patient and physician to oneself. One can even learn to laugh at oneself. One can encourage oneself, try not to take oneself too seriously. Perhaps in one or another respect, one has experienced a disappointment which one should, and also can, bravely swallow without it becoming the starting point of a depression that spreads over an entire life-span.

Look into yourself, and ask yourself why you suffer from your moods, and then you will really have no need to despair. One cannot do everything. One cannot make everything of oneself that one wants to be. But one can slowly become a type of person that, mindful of God, one can at least endure oneself, indeed, even arrive at a certain joy over the kind of person one is as well as over what one does. You are still young and you can emerge from all this a real person not only in the sense of a petty bourgeois, but as a being embodying the standards of an authentic humanism which it is eminently worth the effort to live and to offer to God.

You write that you would be grateful for any answer. Perhaps the answer is not of the kind that merits much gratitude. But just try once more to courageously derive some meaning from these flippant counsels, and then perhaps you will take another long step further along your life's path towards the goal that you have set for yourself.

And I should like to add something more in the manner of a brief postscript. You say that you want to break away from your family. Perhaps in the long run this is necessary if you are to actualize your authentic self-discovery, even though this need not necessarily be the upshot of noisy quarrels and revolutionary upheavals. I suggest that so long as you live with your family for whatever reasons and so long as your family gets on your nerves (as the saying goes), try nevertheless to feel yourself responsible for all of them and try also to pray for them. It is a remarkable fact that if we do not demand so much from others, but recognize that we must also give something and also do give something, our relationship to other people very often fundamentally changes and becomes easier. Pray a little for your parents and your brothers and sisters.

Cordially,

Karl Rahner

THREE

DOES GOD KNOW BEFOREHAND
IF I DO OR I DON'T BELIEVE?

Dear Father Rahner,

I should like to write you a letter on a theme that is of great concern to me, namely the problem of predetermination or predestination.

I have often wondered how I, as a Catholic, stand vis-a-vis this controversial question. I have never found a satisfactory answer to my questions in my reflections, but I would like first of all to relate my thoughts on this matter to you.

What seems most important to me is the question on whether we human beings from the outset are already accepted or rejected through God's predetermination. Or is it only later in life that we decide our attitude vis-a-vis God? I have often heard that God does not compel us to believe in him and to love him. Rather, we are given the option to say "yes" to him. That then would mean that we humans, on our own, can decide according to our free will whether or not to side with God.

This appears to me as quite evident upon a first consideration, but then when I ponder the matter further, the assertion strikes me as somewhat ques-

tionable. In order to make myself more understandable, I should like to cite Judas as an example.
In the New Testament it is often stated that Jesus had
foreknown his way of the cross and known the persons who would bring it about. From that I conclude
that Judas and others were destined by God to play
the part of the "wicked" in Jesus' life.

Did Judas therefore have any choice at all to
become a person other than one who was to betray
Jesus? Are Jesus' enemies of this time capable of
determining whether they are for or against Jesus?

No, not really. There had to be some persons
who came forward as Jesus' enemies, inasmuch as according to the Bible Christ's crucifixion and resurrection of necessity was to come to pass. Hence particular persons were predestined to be Jesus' enemies,
for otherwise there would have been no resurrection.
Perhaps it sounds somewhat odd, but couldn't these
persons just as well have become persons of a different stripe who were for Jesus? In fact, can I now
really decide on my own whether I have a positive or a
negative attitude toward the person of God?

It strikes me sometimes that it would be meaningless if I were to arrive at the conclusion that God
forces me to do something, if he has determined
beforehand whether I would believe in him.

Yet it is also true that God knows and loves us
before we are born. He knows how we will relate to
him once we enter upon existence. Can I, therefore,
on my own still decide whether I am to say "yes" to
the Lord?

I don't know whether my questions are
justifiable. Perhaps I may receive a quite simple
answer to them. These questions strike me as very important.

Very affectionately and with cordial thanks for your help,

Christiane

Dear Christiane,

I found your letter interesting because it gladdens me to know that even in our day there are still persons who occupy themselves with theological questions which, from New Testament times down the centuries, have troubled very lofty minds and have also given rise to violent controversies.

You must not think that there is a really graspable solution to your question. Wherever God comes into question the answer can never be formulated in such a way that upon hearing it we can instantly react with a "Aha, now the matter is crystal clear." Such an answer would surely be wrong for the reason that with our "solution" we would have had to seize and master the incomprehensibleness of God without which he would not really be God. This is how matters stand, inalterably to the end. In such a case it is possible for us to propound several propositions of which we cannot, on the one hand, say with unequivocal clarity that they contradict each other and couple this with the inference that consequently one or the other proposition, or both, must surely be false. On the other hand, however, we still might not clearly grasp the positive compatability of these propositions. Your question will entail such a series of propositions, all of which we cannot give up, despite the fact that we cannot comprehend their positive compatibility and deductibility from a common principle.

Therefore as wise persons and believing Christians we must say: freedom and responsibility are givens in our existence, and we cannot conveniently and easily escape from this responsibility by a reference to God who assertedly "predestined" my behavior. I may not deny God's influence even if, admittedly, I do not exactly know at which particular point of my life this responsibility and freedom of mine are actualized. I am the whole—if I may put it thus—I who am left to my own discretion and who may not expediently dissolve himself in a nest of compulsions and constraints, however much it remains true that there are such inner and outer imperatives in my life to which I remain subject.

Now I must set alongside it a second proposition which I cannot fully understand in the light of the first proposition because it goes beyond my personal responsibility, namely the proposition that the infinite, incomprehensible God exists. The second (a long one) proposition can be formulated as follows:

God, in his infinite freedom, also knows the history of my freedom. In its earthly life it stands constantly before his simple eternity (you see, I am trying to avoid the word "beforehand"). This wisdom of God that belongs to his simple eternity, to his simple "eternal now" does not annul my freedom. As something finite for which I am inescapably responsible, this freedom of mine is and remains encompassed not only by this knowledge of God, but also by his creative power. My freedom is borne by this power—in the good deeds as well as the wicked deeds that I commit to the extent that this wickedness is still a positive reality which, in order to be, requires the creative power of God. So we are by no means predestined in the sense of a coercion and of a compulsion or necessity of a kind that would annul our freedom. Insofar as in our being and deeds (also in our free deeds), something is real and thus good (even in our wicked deeds), we must once more accept this reality of ours and even the deeds of our freedom in thanks to God as the gift of his creative power and of his loving grace because once again my ultimate, ir- reducible reality, identified with me, even as free, is also his gift. This birth of all my reality from God does not annul me either in my reality or in my real freedom, but, rather, grounds both.

God and my reality and freedom are not com- petitors between whom one, as it were, must make a complete division. All is from him but all that thus comes from him has at its apex this quality of God himself (naturally only analogously): the freedom and thus the capability to be love.

Surely I must have now propounded proposi- tions of which you will probably say: I don't see how all this fits together. Well, neither do I see how all this could stand positively in a transparent harmony. But as a thinking man and as a Christian I admit that I cannot and should not comprehend all this positively in terms of its compatibility. Rather, I must let these propositions humbly remain alongside each other in their plurality and thus, adoringly, I do homage to God's incomprehensibleness.

In a certain sense one can say: only the Christian can really manage to let God be God, without want- ing to capture him and fix him as a definite point in a system of coordinates established by us. Insofar as I experience freedom and take upon myself a res- ponsibility that I may not shrug off, and insofar as I, at the same time, also experience, believe in and ac- cept God as the incomprehensibleness of my ex- istence, I have altogether sufficient right to assert and maintain each of these propositions. At the same time

I see that it would be wrong to reject the one or the other proposition only because I cannot positively perceive its compatibility with the other. Neither do I have the right, in a crowning act of intellectual arrogance, to build a system out of these propositions that I myself should try to control.

It occurs to me at this point that Christian philosophies and theologians, here and there, have often succumbed to the danger of over-stepping these limits set to creaturely thinking and sought to know more than is possible as regards the compatibility of such propositions. I cannot in such a brief letter point out what I consider such over-stepping of limits in the different Christian systems. That would probably only bore you and actually be unnecessary for your religious life. I think, however, that it is really wonderful when one experiences that the reality of God and of the world is deeper and more incomprehensible than suspected, too much so for it to be simply mentally mastered.

It is true that one can cope with the incomprehensibleness of God when one does not try to master him mentally, but rather loves him. This obtains more than ever in the matter of human love. When a person would love another only in that which he or she has comprehended of the other wherein this other corresponds to the ideals and wishes fashioned by oneself, then one has not really loved the other. One must accept the other, as he or she is in himself or herself and for himself or herself. Only thus, only in such a love, can we really succeed in finding the other in his or her inmost reality. The same holds true with regard to God and his incomprehensibleness.

Perhaps you will now say that I should have applied all these problems to concrete cases of salvation history and its opposite, and that I should have said something about Jesus' enemies who without prejudice to their freedom and culpable responsibility, were inserted by God in God's positive salvation plan without, for this reason, being able to justify themselves before God. It is true that God can let even those who seek and love him incline to wickedness, in the exercise of their human freedom, and others to salvation and grace. Paul has already stressed this point (look for the passage yourself in the letter to the Romans!) and, nevertheless, he declared that no one may deduce the right to commit this wickedness in the exercise of a freedom that God utilizes for the salvation of others.

Many greetings and cordial best wishes! I hope you experience joy in your freedom—as one challenged to accomplish the deed of your freedom just as much as one who entrusts herself and her not wholly comprehensible freedom hopefully and trustfully to the love of God.

Karl Rahner

FOUR

GRATEFUL TO GOD, WITH SO MUCH MISERY IN THE WORLD?

Dear Father Rahner,

First of all, I should like to say that I am especially proud to be able to write to you. I have heard or read very much about you and know something about your importance for the Church and for all Christians. So it is quite understandable that I was greatly pleased with your visit and the Mass that you celebrated with us. Let me also thank you for your kindness to me: I am the one to whom you gave the opera ticket.

In our youth group there is a "social work circle" with which I have become involved. What I do there is in principle quite simple: my basic assignment is to attend to an isolated person in an old age home. I visit him once a week.

For me the encounter with old people was a great challenge since up to the time I started this, I had had hardly anything to do with them (I see my grandparents at most three times a year, because they live pretty far away). This encounter was also an emotional moving experience. It was often the point of departure for a series of reflections and (even more often) of questions . . . of which I have become acutely conscious for the first time. It was with a great deal of idealism (I wanted to bring these people some variety, conversation, verve and joy) that I went there the first time. But this idealism was soon dampened—the whole climate, the whole atmosphere there were terribly depressing. Each inmate was so apathetic. Even when I made an effort to smile at someone, I was merely stared at in return, indifferently. The old age home as such is a massive structure and there each inmate must appear to himself or herself as just a number among four thousand others.

For a year I have been attending to a certain Frau M. She is nearly eighty, and has been in the old age home for six years and bed-ridden almost all of the time because she is paralyzed in both legs. Nevertheless in her own way she is still one of the most agile persons in her room. At first, I was always repeatedly disappointed to note the slight importance that she seemingly attached to my visit. Her reaction was always one ranging from distrust to indifference. But the longer I had contact with her and the deeper our relationship became, the more I arrived at a somewhat different conclusion: that she (and probably also most of the others) was deeply embittered because of the goings on there. This was probably the result of their ages but, above all, this bitterness stemmed from their often deep great personal sufferings. It was also the cause of many, often childish quarrels among themselves. No doubt this was also the reason why patients who sometimes have lain beside each other for eight years hardly ever speak to each other out of sheer mistrust. Another consequence of this bitterness was precisely an indifference terrible to behold.

On the same evening I go to a prayer circle. We sing very beautiful hymns of the nearness and love of God and so many there give thanks for something that occurred during the day just past. However, I found it very difficult to give thanks. I could, of course, give thanks for my life—things are going well with me. But how can I really give thanks when at the same time I find myself constantly thinking of the question that the (very devout) old woman once posed to me: "Why must I suffer all that when throughout my whole life I really took great pains so to live as God wanted me to? Why doesn't God let me die—I just want to have an end put to this whole life?"

On one occasion I intensely experienced all that: in the interval between the visit to the old age home and the prayer circle I briefly watched a news program on TV—an earthquake had taken many lives. After that I simply could not sing along with the others—all that suddenly struck me as a dreamily beautiful but enormously dishonest wishful ideal in an imaginary safe and sound world.

Dear Father Rahner, I should like you to help me overcome this contradiction.

Cordial greetings,

Alexander

Dear Alexander,

First of all let me say that I think it's splendid that you go to this old age home and undergo shattering experiences of human life and its abysses before which most of your peers slink away. You won't always be able to be a volunteer in such an institution, but meanwhile you are doing something really Christian and, at the same time, are learning much about Christian life for when you are a grown-up.

I cannot, of course, now write on the whole problem of this old age home where so many old people are squeezed together. But it is precisely when you tell yourself that such conditions ought not to be, when you experience that you, too, cannot change anything, that you are set before the task of reflecting and of experiencing how one, as a Christian, can cope with such unfathomable dimensions of life which should not exist and which cannot be removed from the world. I would prefer not to write on this matter. When you think of the cross of Christ, you actually have the most radical case of this fundamental life-problem and also the only solution that is realistic and horrible and yet signifies a blessed denouement.

In this old age home you come in contact with many old people who are simply old, perhaps also blamelessly embittered, and who (to put it mildly) are at times senile. Consider always, at the same time, that such sufferings and bitternesses are indeed terrible but that, then, when they no longer have anything to do with personal fault (don't be alarmed by this assertion) they are more inoffensive before God and find their solution easier in eternal life than do transgressions that really constitute fault and sin and that are committed and yielded to, almost as a matter of course, in times of good health. The last problems are precisely those of the possible real guilt before God (and naturally also the sufferings and misfortunes springing up from them).

The Christian finds that difficult to grasp and to take seriously, but that's just the way it is. Now you ask me how God can allow so much suffering that you so palpably experience in this old age home. I once wrote an article with the title "How Can God Let Us Suffer?" In this brief letter, I think I should refer you to this article which ought to be obtainable if you inquire about it in your parish. In this article, too, the only answer I give to the question posed by you and an old woman is that I cannot answer the question. That, despite all justified and meaningful partial answers, in the final analysis, it is unanswerable and is part of the incomprehensible mystery of God himself. It escapes us so that the hopeful acceptance of our suffering is but the concrete way in which we lovingly accept the eternal incomprehensibleness of God himself.

Man is (I don't know whether at sixteen you can to a certain extent understand this) specifically the being who cannot in mind and heart rest content with what he grasps and perceives—no matter how beautiful and magnificent this may be. And when he tries to reach beyond that, man unfailingly comes up against the incomprehensibleness of God. Then the question that poses itself is whether he can muster the improbable courage of a love that is convinced that the love of the no longer comprehensible God is man's true and, in the end, sole blessedness. In view of the real suffering in the world he can achieve this courage, of course, only from a strength that comes from God.

If you in this old age home have experienced how these old, troubled people living in close quarters can no longer muster up a courage of this kind—which does not seem difficult to your youthful idealism—then just consider that these protests, complaints, resistances which seem to characterize these people at the terminus of their lives are not at all real personal happenings for which they will bear responsibility before God.

If someone, for example, is pierced by a blazing hot iron, then even the holiest man screams. Only he is so confounded that he can no longer think of God, he is simply swallowed up by the torment of his pain. His love of God was actualized in the earlier phases of his life, at moments when this person, in freedom and self-possession, was alone and delivered himself to the mystery of God.

Such will often also be the case with these old people. They perhaps cannot realize any relationship to God in freedom. We may trust in the supposition, however, that they did this once at an earlier time and that this essential life-deed has been accepted by God.

When an old person up to the moment of his or her death still possesses the inner clearness and freedom—that really happens and it is not infrequent—to realize his or her personal relationship to God (as I know from a fellow-Jesuit) that just to pray "in the name of the Father and of the Son and of the Holy Spirit" and to die with these words as such is glorious and a grace of God. But when you undergo the experience of watching vexed and bitter human beings who are no longer capable of that, it is bound, nevertheless, to be a bitter and difficult experience to bear in your life—as are all experiences of the incomprehensible suffering in the world. Nevertheless it is an experience that must not unnerve you in a last-ditch Christian optimism as to the meaning of life. Such persons have already for a long time been embraced by a silent love of God.

All best wishes to you, for your work in the old age home and in the parish community.

Karl Rahner

FIVE

MY BIGGEST BOTTLENECK IS PRAYER

Dear Father Rahner,

Daily I ask myself questions that often remain unanswered, partly because I am too lazy to ponder them because I have never been able to come up with an answer to them on my own. Prayer, conducting a conversation with the good God, is my biggest bottleneck. It is surely not enough to act only according to God's demands and wishes, that is, strictly speaking, according to God's commandments. To be sure, prayer for other persons, for myself and for life is also very important. But most of the time I can't manage to turn away from the daily grind, from the many mini and maxi cares and to converse with God. It is positively alarming how during evening prayer I am always so easily diverted and arrive at other thoughts so that the prayer sometimes stretches out to a half hour. Of this time I sacrifice, perhaps, only ten minutes to the Lord. I find it discouraging inasmuch as I have already tried many changes—for example, to recite only shorter prayers, only an *Our Father* or so. But soon the laxity again becomes greater than the idealism and today the situation is as it was before.

Naturally I am grateful to the good God for the many things that he has given to me and to all others and continues to give. During the day I often think of him with gratitude but as soon as I once set aside time for prayer, or when I sit in a cool church and try to express my gratitude for my relationship with God I lose myself in meaningless words. For example, I often simply say unconsciously: "Dear God, help me!" although everything with me is going quite well. I don't know whether the good God is pleased with my prayer. I am also certain that it could be better—but how? How can I forget laxity, laziness and inconsistency? How can I learn to pray?

I already imagine to myself that for God prayer must be immensely important. In every friendship personal conversation counts most of all. It is precisely for this reason that my inability to pray correctly is so depressing to me. But in my inmost being I hope and trust in God who at some moment or other will bestow an "illumination" on me.

Many, many grateful greetings,

John

Dear John,

Actually what you write about yourself and your life of prayer is wonderful and not at all so grave as to call for the stern sentence that you pass on yourself and your praying. You do pray, after all. Whether it be an *Our Father* or a long prayer, the difference is not so important. Even if one simply says, "Dear God, help me!" that is already splendid. In so doing, one need not know exactly how God is going to help one when everything is going quite well. This is especially true if the actual prayer is preceded by a rather long time of reflection during which you are concerned with yourself and all that happens. During such a meditation one reflects first of all on God, on one's own obligations and tasks, cares and needs, and then reflection slowly flows into a real prayer. With all this, of course, I am not saying that you couldn't learn to pray better! You can and must do that, naturally. No one, so long as one lives, and one's life has not yet entered into the eternal face to face praise of God, will have succeeded in voicing prayer in its loftiest and most perfect form. In this matter, we always remain novices.

There are many methods on how one can learn to pray better because prayer, however much it be God's gift and grace, nevertheless also has human psychological presuppositions which must be taken into consideration if one really wants to pray. Just as in other spiritual matters one must slowly learn concentration, ways to focus attention on spiritual realities, such an acquired skill as "collectedness" during prayer must also be learned. One must, on the one hand, effect a real distance from the superficial business of one's life and, on the other, one must also learn to take this manifold of thoughts, tasks, cares, disappointments, joys etc. along with one to God and to "gather" them, so to speak.

Beyond that there are many simple methods designed to facilitate and improve prayer. Such "tricks" are listed in St. Ignatius of Loyola's book of spiritual exercises. Read them yourself! Try for once to dwell on the single words of a prayer that you have learned by heart, to elucidate, to develop the content of such single words. Such meditative reflection should naturally flow into a personal prayer to God. As crazy as this may sound in our day, I would nevertheless recommend that for once you try to pray the rosary for yourself alone. The restful, relaxed, spoken succession of the same words and a glimpse into the mysteries of the life of Jesus invoked in it can, if one in so doing does not become impatient but tries to slowly train oneself properly, call forth that particular stillness in one which brings a person to God.

Finally spiritual directors know very well that genuine prayer does not ultimately depend on the differentiated fullness of the thoughts proposed to the good God, and in the very final analysis not even on the manifold of petitions and wishes with which one tries to attract, as it were, God (even if "prayer is immensely important to us and not specifically to God"). Rather, it depends on a collected stillness (may one even say emptiness?) in which the whole person, trustfully and lovingly, embosoms himself or herself to the silent mystery of God. Just as skiing cannot be learned through theoretical lectures, but one must actually ski in order to learn the sport. And just as in skiing one must always pick oneself up again if at first one falls down, so it is also with prayer. Prayer can be learned only through prayer.

It has been very clear from your letter that you do pray. Don't give it up. Always begin again. You have begun and with patience you will always learn to do it better. When one interprets repeatedly and rightly the new experiences of one's life, these new experiences always occasion a new way, unknown up to then, to appear prayerfully before God. To take the new in one's life in prayer to God, whether it consists of blissful or terrible experiences, palpable blessings or even bitter disappointments over oneself, to make everything in life actually become prayer: this is prayer and one learns to pray by praying.

Thank you for sending me your youth magazine. It's splendid that you participate so selflessly and diligently in the service of your group. Take these concerns and needs that are reported in this magazine along with you in your prayer before God and at the same time you can even give a thought to the one who has written you this letter.

With cordial greetings.

Karl Rahner

SIX

WHEN EVERYDAY LIFE BECOMES A TORMENT

Dear Father Rahner,

First of all I should like to thank you most sincerely for being given a chance to write you. That made me feel a little happier than usual since I have learned very much about you. Now I am writing you simply on how things stand with me.

My present situation is the worst conceivable. Why, I myself do not exactly know. At all events, I often reflect on death. And, to be honest, I find thinking upon it lots of fun. I have no fear of death and am really quite curious about it. Perhaps my attitude stems from the fact that I have been reading a great deal of Hermann Hesse. He expounds his total relationship and sadness as something altogether positive.

The holiday season has just come to a close. At the moment I live only on memories and sit even deeper in shit than before the holidays. The drinking sprees are even worse because one has nothing to do and because my classmates constantly urge me on. I don't withstand the temptation for long, and then something happens.

I have had a total falling out with my parents and the only person who has remained friendly to me is N. Up to now we have been seeing each other every weekend. But her parents are pretty mean. They allow N. to stay out only until 9 and think that visiting her every week is all too much. If only they knew what they were doing with all this strictness. And N. is very dependent on her parents. She must obey. And in the face of all this one is not supposed to despair and doubt!

Why all this? What's the point of it? For me everyday life has become a torment. The longing for a place of shelteredness and love is vigorously oppressed and blocked from all sides in this world.

You live for your faith and I admire and envy you for that. I am sorry that I have yet found this faith, although I actively strive to do so. I have doubts about everything, especially about myself. I live with dreams and not with reality. I am an idealist on a human level. But should I give up these ideals merely because reality teaches me something different? No, I would prefer to perish for my ideals rather than give them up.

You probably already know that last week a class-mate, whom I liked very much and with whom I enjoyed a good understanding, shot himself. Since then I've been terribly depressed. Often both of us had talked about suicide and actually discussed it at length. And now he has carried it out. I cried like a child at his burial. But perhaps now he feels alright and is probably better off than before.

Believe me, Father, when I heard about it I had no other thought than to do likewise. But there is still someone, perhaps the only person that I genuinely love. It would be shabby to do that now. But in such moments each one is closest, above all, to oneself. At one time I even considered whether I shouldn't terminate my relationship with N. in order to have "a clear road ahead.''

You probably will not understand me. I myself don't know whether I should have written you all this. Nevertheless I must ask you, please try to understand me and my attitude. So I wait for an answer.

Many thanks for taking the trouble to reply, and cordial greetings,

Robert

Dear Robert,

I must first of all confess that I let your letter be around for a long time. I shouldn't have done that. But that's the way it is. If, as a result, you have experienced another disappointment, this time with me, neither can that be changed and I can only ask you to reflect on this disappointment too. Add it to the others that you describe in your letter and then make an effort to cope with all of them.

I hope that in the meantime much has changed through the education that life itself bestows on us. Hopefully you have learned something from the death of your friend and drawn the right conclusions. The right one is not to toy with the thought of suicide. You have nothing to judge in your friend as regards his act because every death in a human being is a mystery that we cannot fathom. Your death in any case is different from that of your friend. Were you to try to run away from yourself in such a way, it would be an act of cowardice which does not solve any life-problem but merely finalizes it.

Moreover I should like, quite soberly and primitively, to say: "Cut out the drinking sprees" (hopefully you've already done so!). Don't experience your relationship to your parents as an affliction calling for self-commiseration but as an enjoined task that you yourself must master. Parents are often limited human beings, quite obviously. But that is no reason for you to have a "falling out" with them. Rather, see it as another task in which you yourself must learn to acquire understanding and patience with others. And to look for the blame of dissensions in yourself through a self-critical reckoning with the fact that one also makes one's own particular contribution to these quarrels.

Perhaps you have already resolved your problem with N. by yourself. Is such an assumption wholly wide of the mark? Should such be the case, the new experience should not occasion you to blithely forget the past as if it were merely a matter of changes that come and go like the weather. Ask yourself if you have really learned something from such experiences and, accordingly, if you knew yourself better so as not to be taken in by the first access of feeling or short-circuited longing for shelteredness that may come along. Were N.'s parents really so "mean" if your feeling for the girl has again changed and you, at bottom, are happy to have a "clear road ahead." One must have the courage really to learn from one's experiences. Then they can afterward change into "blessed blunders" which one judges mildly but which one does not again commit with exactly the same stupidity as before which unfortunately most do.

I don't know whether I've really understood you. But you were right to commit all that to writing even though I am far from having answered everything to which you have made allusions. Keep on trying courageously to arrive at the faith which you think you have not yet found. If you do this you will at least have a living faith in embryo. And you should not give up your "ideals" because it is in them that your true reality inheres, and not in that which persons who are cowardly, short-sighted and smug view as reality.

You say that you admire me for my faith. That's no simple matter with me either. In the final analysis I must also strive daily for my own faith, just as I have recommended this striving to you. And if I, perhaps, at my age have the impression as regards myself and others that it is easier for me to embrace than for young people, then I must tell myself that this agility perhaps is not a witness of a greater faith but only the consequence of a certain calcination which sets in with age. There is no exact knowledge on such a matter.

You and I must still learn the faith in the eternal God, in whose infinite breadth and incomprehensibleness all our problems have their definite place and indeed precisely when we ourselves do not know how this will come to pass.

Cordial greetings,

Karl Rahner

SEVEN

I DON'T NEED A CHURCH IN ORDER
TO LOVE GOD

Dear Father Rahner,

It's best I begin by getting directly to the point. After long reflection I have come to believe in God, but not in the Church. But I cannot easily substantiate why. It's in part because the Church, in my opinion, has a "black" past (consider the Middle Ages), in part because I can come closer to God even without the Church and pray to God also without necessarily attending Mass. This for me is the guiding goal. It almost disgusts me to watch people recite in a sing-song manner a prayer that they have memorized or rehearsed without paying attention to its meaning. This is why I find it laughable to pray the rosary as I see no meaning in it except perhaps as a way of attuning oneself to the Mass or to God. Could not one recite a recipe in exactly the same way?

I feel exactly the same way about going to confession. It has no meaning for me because I don't believe that a priest merely by uttering a few words—and as "penance" a prayer—can "forgive" my sins. This way I could sin round the clock and then have myself "forgiven." Why should I not bear the "consequences" of my sins inasmuch as I have committed them? To let myself be forgiven by a human being is after all only a sign of my fear of appearing before God with my sins and to have to really atone for them. Unfortunately, unlike so many others, I don't have the strength really to atone for them during my life-time so I must wait to do so after my death.

Moreover, I am not in agreement with all the rituals of the Church since I believe that an authentic believer does not need symbolic actions for his faith. I also remember reading once in the Bible that one should not station oneself ostentatiously on a street corner or in a synagogue to pray. After these words, which I find very reassuring, comes the *Our Father,* and I find this passage to be the most important in the New Testament.

Sometimes I also believe that I may be wrong and I doubt the conclusions I draw from my reflections. And then I wish that I had a staunch faith in God and in the Church. Hopefully you may be able to help me to understand the Church so that I may cease viewing it so negatively. It would interest me to know what you think about all this.

Awaiting—hopefully—a reply, I remain most cordially yours,

Gregory

Dear Gregory,

I read your letter (I confess it gladly) with a certain pleasure and sometimes laughter. If you think that one could just as well recite a recipe as well as pray the rosary, then I must assure you that you have never prayed a rosary. Had you actually ever tried to do so it might have perhaps dawned on you that in the very monotony of this prayer—apart from the essence of the prayer as such—you are suffused with an enormous strength in calm, in relaxation, in courage, far from the hustle and bustle of everyday life. But all that is incidental.

Actually I wonder why you young people have such great difficulties with the Church. Today you all incline, in contrast to us old individualists of the past or of a vanishing time, to something that one could call "socialism" (rightly understood). Young people today want community, they demand closeness with one another, brotherliness, service to the neighbor. If, however, a community is to avoid the self-dissolution that sooner or later is the fate of like-minded groups and, instead, provide an enduring foundation for a person and his or her life, then it requires structure, and indeed unavoidably, organized community structures and discipline, as well as much unselfishness from individuals.

I find it singular that you want to be socialists and yet cannot summon up any understanding of the Church. It is after all a community in which there exist, naturally, duties, regulations, norms to which one must adapt oneself with a certain unselfishness. Naturally it is only when one does that freely, easily and honorably that one also finds the blessing that such a community can give one. It is something similar to what transpires in a family. One can experience its shelteredness, its reciprocal help only when one unquestioningly renders the services that such an association unavoidably enjoins and requires.

I have often heard people say that they can approach God even without a Church, that they find him in nature, etc. Obviously a Christian cannot doubt that each one who obeys his or her conscience in selfless fidelity ultimately can find God. But can the situation not also be so that a conscience open to reality and its plenitude precisely perceives that the community of the Church is also a demand that God poses to one through this very conscience? Can the situation not also be such that one, through and with the Church, comes closer more radically, more selflessly to the infinite God, that one undergoes experiences with God which after all one can undergo only in the Church?

Is the situation then really such that one, if he or she is in the Church and lives with it, must recite a prayer in a "sing-song manner," and mechanically list one's sins in order to obtain forgiveness? Isn't the situation really otherwise in that whoever really, believingly grasps the significance of the Eucharist experiences in this holy happening a nearness to Christ Jesus, his life, his death on the Cross and his resurrection which he or she cannot find otherwise? Can one not place oneself in an authentic and personal way in the choir of those who pray?

One can, of course, as a wholly normal Christian freely attend that religious service, participate in that prayer community, that celebration of the Eucharist that lies closer to one personally and creates less difficulties perhaps than are occasioned by the religious service in some other parish community. But it is simply unjust to dismiss what transpires in the religious service of the Church as a laughable sing-song recital of prayer. Are you in your own life, as a matter of course, in such an undisputed oneness and community with the holy God of eternal life that you have no need for Jesus' word of forgiveness through the mediation of the Church? I must honestly say that

I found your statement: "An authentic believer does not need symbolic actions for his faith" frightfully silly.

Are you a human being compounded of body and soul? Must not the inmost reality at the core of your personality necessarily also express itself externally in embodied events? Can you renounce art and music? After all what transpires in them are but symbolic actions in which a human being expresses the inmost happenings of his or her existence. Why should it be otherwise in the dimension of our relationship to God? A demonstrative prayer on a street corner certainly doesn't belong to the necessary and meaningful embodiment of our relationship to God, especially when it happens merely to display conspicuously one's piety before others (which Jesus rebukes).

It is also silly to assert that Jesus' utterance against such conspicuous display of one's piety is the most important saying in the New Testament. Such an assertion obviously contradicts the intent of Jesus who in his sayings obviously cannot always enunciate the very last and most decisive word at one and the same time in regard to what moves him to speak in a particular context. When Jesus says that one must love God with his whole heart and with all one's strength, for Jesus, obviously, that is a more important saying than that which you declare to be the most important utterance in the New Testament as far as you are concerned. To be sure someone could assert that the totality of what moves Jesus to make pronouncements and of what he wants to bring closer to us repeatedly lies in all Jesus' sayings even when they are pronounced in isolated contexts or situations. But this again changes nothing in the fact that the quintessence of Jesus' message is given in different ways and intensities along with a different urgency and almightiness.

Naturally, in what I have said, to which I cannot add very much more in a brief letter, I have still in no way fully described the real and ultimate essence of the church. But if human beings are always human beings and, of necessity are human beings who live in community, and if there are human beings who believe in Jesus as the person through whom alone, when all is said and done, they come to God and hear his last word of salvation, of forgiveness, of grace and of eternal life, then there must unquestionably be a community of those congregated around Jesus, then there simply must be a Church.

Accordingly one must learn to give with patience, with kindness, with readiness and not only take, and thus grow into the life of this community of faith around Jesus. Try it for once!

You say you wish you had so firm a faith in the Church as you have in God. Basically you don't at all need exactly the same faith, that is to say the absolute identification of yourself with this Opposite, the Church, as you have with your faith vis-a-vis God. For the Church is not God and the last absolute devotion and self-identification which our existence demands is something we have only with regard to God. But just as there also are in other respects realities outside and near God toward which we must have a positive relationship—precisely also because this is enjoined by God—so must we (and we can) also seek and find a positive relationship to the Church.

Try with patience to be self-critical toward yourself, don't consider the experiences that you have had up to now with the Church as exhaustive and final. Just as when one person and another at first have very few good experiences together and then one slowly realizes what a remarkable person the other is, how helpful, how loyal—things can also take such a turn regarding the Church. You yourself say that you sometimes believe that you may be wrong and that you doubt the conclusions that you yourself draw from your own reflections. If that is true, then you are actually on the right path. It could lead you closer to the Church.

I greet you, too, most cordially

Karl Rahner

EIGHT

ANXIETY BEFORE EACH
AND EVERY DECISION

Dear Father Rahner,

A problem that poses itself to me—a seventeen year old girl—is the following: I should like to be able to be accountable for every act, every decision of mine and still feel pleased with myself after such decisions. But, on the one hand, my indolence prevents me from taking such a step and afterwards I try to justify myself with excuses. At one time, after a long day at school, I say to myself that I'm too tired to lend any kind of a hand in the household, and at another time I think to myself: why should I in particular do that? This conceivably could be countered by the question: "Why shouldn't I do that?" Yet this latter question will never occur to me at such moments. I am not approachable and I am wholly entangled in my egoism.

On the other hand—and that is a point that weighs heavily on me—there is in me a measure of cowardice, indeed fear, which means that sometimes I do or say things just because the group also speaks and does likewise. At such moments I simply do not have the courage to confess that I am of an utterly different opinion or that I will not do something because I do not consider it good or proper. It has already often happened to me that, although I had the right answer on the tip of my tongue, I nevertheless said something entirely different.

At all events I always know when I have done or said something wrong. And this knowledge oppresses me and announces itself as my bad conscience. In many decisions I have the sensation of a great weight that bears down on me, that drives me. Before I am overwhelmed, so to speak, I must first come to a decision. Sometimes a right push comes from within and I manage to pull myself together and do what is proper. When, however, I make a wrong decision, I feel uncomfortable, almost as if caught in a trap that has snapped. The pressure to make a decision and the feeling of being harnessed between a wrong and right decision does me in. At the same time, in principle, I always have the will to do the right thing, only at times the will is not strong enough and I am lacking in guidelines.

I think that you, dear Father Rahner, can help me on the basis of your own life experience. I should like to be free of this inhuman pressure and be able to make right decisions.

I wish you all the best and remain gratefully,

Barbara

Dear Barbara,

To tell the truth, I don't really believe that you are living under an "inhuman pressure." Naturally in our manner of life and in our association with other people we must over and over again instantly decide as to what we say or do not say, what we do or do not do. And it is also natural that afterwards—if we are honest and self-critical—we tell ourselves that this or that was not rightly said or done. Such matters in our manner of living should not be viewed as trivial or innocuous or blithely excused. But when after the event, we faultily assess such blunders and allow them to lead to bouts of depression as an after-effect, it is not so much a sign of our moral striving as it is the effect of a false pride that compels us, erroneously, to take our bungling culpably on ourselves. In sum, perhaps, one shouldn't take any relatively unimportant boner of everyday life too seriously.

You should, of course, also pitch in at home and not excuse yourself on the grounds of tiredness in situations where you are quite rightly expected to lend a hand. Such petty faults can be considered and taken seriously in terms of the question of whether they are the effect of an egoism that is at once secret and hidden. And this is really to be taken seriously. But to repeat, one should not allow oneself to be overly weighed down by the deficiencies, indeed even by the petty acts of meanness of our life.

You are not caught in a trap that has snapped, as you put it. But if you calmly and cheerfully judge yourself, you should always say, and be convinced of it, that this trap at bottom is an open one. If today you failed to say a kind word to one of the persons around you, you can at least make up for it tomorrow. If you are now depressed and leave chores to others, make amends for your neglect at the very next opportunity. That you certainly can do and if you repeatedly awaken such a will anew, you ought not to take your earlier lapses and shortcomings so tragically and just attribute many of them to what we weak and short-sighted human beings repeatedly find ourselves doing in the way of daily mistakes and misjudgments.

One falls, but then one lifts oneself up again. If one has been neglectful, there is a way to make up for it. The patience that we owe to our fellow-creatures is something that we also owe to ourselves, and this, too, is a Christian virtue. One must be self-compassionate, just as one is enjoined to be compassionate with others and their weaknesses.

Be serene and joyful and don't take yourself seriously. We must be answerable for our life. But there is also much in our life for which we actually cannot be accountable. We cannot neatly separate the one from the other and naturally, therefore, maintaining an attitude of earnest self-responsibility and self-compassion are two virtues difficult to separate and to distinguish. To practice them jointly remains a singular yet cheerful task of our life and one to be confidently and trustfully accepted.

With all good wishes,

Karl Rahner

NINE

THE PRISON OF INTERNALIZED CONFORMITY

Dear Father Rahner,

I must say from the start that my life actually unfolds very happily and I don't have to grapple with weighty problems. Perhaps, I think to myself, this is the very reason why I brood on so many matters. I should like to write you about something that particularly occupies my thoughts now.

I have been giving some attention to the life of St. Francis of Assisi and his way of life has simply filled me with enthusiasm: the happiness that he experienced in his poverty, his union with God that was all the stronger since he lived in the middle of nature. He himself was at one with nature, like the lillies in the field and the birds on the trees. He lived with Scripture and drew strength from the wondrous purity of his life. What upsets me is that we, that I, am not able to break out of the standardized way of life in order, like him, to set out on a different path, a hard one and perhaps a difficult one at the beginning. Many of us are, no doubt, open to his teachings, but we do not allow ourselves to be really swept up by them to the point of following him. By this I don't mean that we should all join the Franciscan Order.

Rather, I mean following him in his breaking out of the prison of internalized conformity, in the fulfillment and clarity that marked his activity, in his trust in God.

The excuse that today we are living in a wholly different time may perhaps be acceptable, but the problem posed by the new and the fear in front of the new has remained. Francis of Assisi successfully faced the problem and the fear and overcame both.

I realize that I, too, can set out on a new path in little ways, and I need not necessarily and ruthlessly tear myself away entirely from everybody. Nevertheless it saddens me a little to realize that such a step is simply out of the question, that I just can't drop everything for the simple purpose of devoting myself on a broader scale to the pursuit of the real essential matters of my life.

Many thanks for having followed my train of thoughts.

And many cordial greetings,

Marianne

Dear Marianne,

Thanks be to God that you have no burdensome problems and also that you do not artificially torment yourself as do many people who think that only by so doing can one be considered, in one's own view or that of others, a modern-day person possessed of great depth. Francis of Assisi was a wonderful human being, a real Christian, a saint. There are many who contend that after Jesus, he is actually the greatest person in the Church and in the kingdom of heaven. But every human being has the life task intended for him or her by God. Each is a unique individual and

Christian and for this reason one, obviously, cannot simply wish to copy St. Francis.

Whether you, too, are called to a poverty similar to that of this Saint, whether you can live in such an immediate proximity to nature like Francis, whether you can follow Jesus in the style of the Saint with such devout simplicity (i.e. with regard to the peculiarities of Jesus' life, that particularly struck and impressed Francis and that, after all, did not encompass all and everything that Jesus lived) is a question that I, of course, cannot answer and that most likely must be answered with a No rather than with a Yes.

You do indeed live in a time different from that of Francis, your historical and personal situation places you before tasks different from those that were laid upon him. To be sure, we can allow ourselves to be shamed by the radicalness with which the saint lived the imitation of Christ, the Crucified One. To be sure, he can serve as a model so that one may guard oneself against taking over, in an ultimately non-believing matter of course way, the life-style of one's ambience with its superficiality and profaneness. He certainly has something to say to us. But the specific, perhaps radical "alternative" life-style that really is uniquely ours must be found on our own, by ourselves. In a somewhat solemn tone, one might say: "You should not become a St. Francis, but a St. Marianne." What that exactly means, I don't know, of course. You should not be saddened over the fact that your life style is not so simple and cannot be considered to be as simple as the life style such as you fancy you can discern in Francis.

It could be that you can slowly discern your own way, and step by step. You should not always try, impatiently, to avoid the strenuous effort that such an ever to be renewed quest entails. Nor should it sadden you "a little" because things don't move along simply and smoothly without a hitch. I have been in my Order now for almost 60 years and I try to properly fulfill the obligations attendant upon such a way of life to a certain extent. But the concrete path along which I am enjoined to proceed must always be found anew every day.

Finally we mortals are not beings who can structure a life according to their own ideals. Rather, we are beings who in the circumstances of everyday life must let the true life of grace and of freedom be bequeathed to us by God.

Carry on, cheerfully!

I hear that you only recently solemnly received the sacrament of confirmation. By this God's promise has also been tangibly tendered to you in the sphere of the Church so that if your heart remains willing, you will be guided by God's spirit even though you don't possess an exact map of this path through life along which you are enjoined to proceed.

I wish you the best,

Karl Rahner

TEN

PARALYZED BY MY DARK MOODS

Dear Father Rahner,

The faith interests me but I am unable to derive from it as much as others (for example, those in our parish). I believe in God, but less in that Jesus was his son, and the Church together with its organization, values and practice appears to me as altogether questionable. Christians often strike me like little lambs who at times, out of fear of themselves but mostly as a result of the general repression of the inner struggle which everyone must endure until his or her end, mindlessly seek a support. My conception of things is different.

My aim was, and has always remained, the effort to maintain my own thinking as free as possible. I would describe my view thus: there exists an angle the first side of which presents Christianity with its teaching: the second side is the knowledge accumulated in the course of time which though it presents a contrary view nevertheless appears clear and intelligible, that is, it gives one altogether the feeling of rightness. My life is only the bisection of the angle or the diagonal between Christian teaching and other ideas. I will always ponder this proposition, or so I believe, because freedom of thought and the possibility to make comparisons should always remain open. So much for the matter of independence.

My 16-year old existence up to now has been free of sorrow, exempt from troubles and hardship. Nevertheless out of an innate tendency I incline toward an extreme melancholia, indeed to the point of utter despair. Moods of all kinds and contradictions generally make me their prisoner. Although I try not to live in an off-beat, eccentric manner exclusively and to retain contact with others and to open my heart and soul to them, I experience a murderous feeling of impersonalness which is bringing me to the brink of a breakdown. The community can easily operate under a Christian banner (no matter how great or loud the claim), and yet ignore desperate calls for help from neighbors.

I ask you to give me a hint or a suggestion so that I can shape my situation along a more life-enhancing direction. I should not like to become a problem-ridden being who drops out of the ranks. So, I drink occasionally. Thoughts of suicide still never degenerate into even more depressive actions. At the moment I live only for art: with the music of Gustav Mahler. I have found the key for effecting my total identification with another human being. I am stirred to the very depths of my being by his tones. He must, so I think, have felt and thought in a way similar to that of my unhinged mind. If I could compose music, his works would be mine in expression and in problem-formulation, apart from the fact that he was a genius and I am not. I even occupy myself with writing—my only safety-valve, in order to make the whole battle intelligible, in order to be able to stick it out in the ongoing struggle. And the things that materialize on paper are harsh, frightful, indeed perverse, images in the manner of Franz Kafka and George Orwell—apart from the deficiencies in craftmanship.

Perhaps I write all this only because our ski-course turned out worse than in the boldest imaginings. As a community-minded person I have again fundamentally failed all along the line, my accursed disposition ever remains an over-heavy burden on me. I get in my own way even as regards the satisfaction of such elementary and important matters like sexuality. Moments of unburdened cheerfulness become ever rarer and one who is in the dumps is hardly in great demand in public. So in the end all that remains is the old solitude with its self-laceration. Frenzied beer-drinking bouts are conscious moments of self-deception.

In closing I should like to add for the sake of completeness that I have a wonderful relationship with my parents, yet despite many, often deep conversations, they have still never wanted to know or perceive my real character. My few friends, likewise, show almost no understanding and the fact that I am not really a quiet person but, on occasion, even rather lively. Outwardly I stand with both feet in life, inwardly I have to struggle. My dream is to have a friend or better a girl-friend on whose lap I can lay my heart cry out loud. Yet this in all remains, and probably forever, a distant dream, like so many.

I could not have been more honest, and it makes me feel good because before others I most often put on a mask in order to come half-way through. Here I can only repeat my request for advice, indeed for genuine help.

Respectfully,

Harold

Dear Harold,

I will immediately confess to you that I feel that your letter makes excessive demands on me. I think that what you write, at the beginning of your letter, on your relationship to Christianity and the Church is not of such importance that I respond to it here and now. Of greater importance is what you have to say in the first part of your letter: what you report of your loneliness with its self-laceration, of your unfulfilled dreams, of the situation that appears to you as an imprisonment, of your eccentricity and lack of contact with others. That matters should thus stand with you even though you have a wonderful relationship with your parents and life, in other respects, outwardly does not unduly bother you, and even though you are intelligent, indeed so much so that you are driven to writing, how can you not help but tell yourself that your situation results from a general depressive innate inclination that in no way depends on the outer and contingent circumstances of your life.

If everything that you relate is an expression of an innate inclination which from the very outset and beforehand clouds your relationship to Christianity on pertinent individual questions, then it is difficult for me to advise you and I feel you are asking me questions too deep for me to answer. What can one say to a person like yourself, what can one advise him? How comfort him? After all one cannot banish your fundamental frame of mind toward life with kind but superficial sounding counsels. Still, can't you honestly admit this situation to yourself? Can't you say: I must for the time being always reckon with this psychological bent of mine even though the possibility that the further development of my life (also in a biological and physiological respect) may lead me to a more cheerful and more joyful disposition and is still far from being definitively determined. But so long as your inner mood is what it is, you must reckon with it cooly and collectedly.

On the other hand, you cannot supinely surrender to this moodiness. Of course, you can't make it go away by waving a magic wand and metamorphose yourself on order into a happy-cheerful fellow. But you can make yours the knowledge that one must not necessarily and ineluctably be as you are, and given such a basic disposition one should draw conclusions bearing on reality only after exercising the sternest self-criticism and the greatest caution. In short, one ought not be the kind of person who asserts that there is no sun because he or she cannot see it on account of the clouds momentarily overhead.

You can patiently work on yourself. You can try to develop the positive side of your basic frame of mind. For such sides do exist. A person so melancholy at the base of his being as you seem to be has quite a number of choices to make something positive out of this innate moodiness. Because of it you cannot bring yourself to live primitively and superficially for the moment (neither, of course, should you find an escape in beer-drinking bouts!). You appreciate Mahler's music. Isn't that a positive talent (that a superficial person doesn't always possess) in your life? You have what is mostly lacking in young people, an obvious appreciation of your parents and of their devotion to you, otherwise you couldn't have described your relationship to them as "wonderful." Isn't that also something really wonderful for which you can be grateful?

You say that you haven't many friends, but perhaps you do find persons to whom a genuine friendship can bind you. At the same time you should not overly yield to a yearning for "a girl-friend on whose lap I can lay my head and cry out loud," etc., because true love, despite all the mutual support it involves still presupposes individuals who stand on their own feet, who boldly master life and who can, on the basis of this very strength and power, be available to and for the other without receiving the other only as a convenient source of consolation for one's own egoism.

So you see that I cannot provide you with any simple trick through which you can make your life merrier and more bearable. But that is also not really necessary. I mean that you should bravely take on the task that your temperament sets before you. I am convinced that you can effectively shape a great and deeply meaningful life out of your disposition. To accomplish this you don't at all have to be an "unhinged mind." You will, of course, with time, also experience that art or music alone cannot offer the ultimate meaning of life, but that you must and can shape a life with God in fidelity.

You say: "I believe in God." Take the statement seriously, fill it with life! Perhaps even then a difficult and earnest life is demanded of you by this God. But also why not? We cannot select our life according to our pleasure and according to the arbitrariness of our problematic whims and wishes. We must accept ourselves as we are. But when we do this really honestly, courageously and hopefully, we accept God himself. But he is not the God who enjoins a despairing feeling of imprisonment from us. He asks from us, perhaps, that we embark on long paths of life on which we must wearily move ever forward, but nevertheless he remains the God of eternal light.

Dear Harold, I am at the end of this letter which is as short and really as perplexed as it was at the beginning. But perhaps this confession, that I must also accept for myself, may be of some help to you on your path. You shouldn't have written "Yours respectfully" at the end of your letter. We Christians are brothers who can honestly confess their perplexities and thus inwardly draw closer to each other. On the basis of this closeness I say to you with good wishes: don't give up, there is no valid reason to let oneself sink into a hopeless and lonely pit of despair.

Karl Rahner

ELEVEN

LIFE IS LIKE STRAGGLING ALONG
A MOUNTAIN PRECIPICE

Dear Father Rahner,

A friend once took me along to a group dis-
cussion hour sponsored by the Catholic Youth
Organization. There I declared that I could not accept
God as a given, that there was no proof for his existence—and that there was none for Jesus as well.
Nobody present could refute the assertion that Jesus
had received his extraordinary attributes only by
chance—and that he had duped mankind. Contrary
to my expectations the people in the group took no
umbrage but accepted me just as I was. So I went
back there often.

During a long hospital stay I had lots of time on
my hands—time enough to reflect on God. (Perhaps
he exists, for I can just as little deny his existence, of
course, on the basis of purely rational
considerations). This period of reflection surely was a
first step toward God and yet I am still very unsure
and still searching. Only the circumstances of
hospitalization led me to concern myself somewhat
more closely with "Christian matters." One can certainly observe that illness and material poverty are a

propitious fertile soil for faith. And the Catholic Church understands, and masterfully so, how to transmit faith to such persons and thereby provide a prop for them. I feel that I belong to a different breed of persons: persons of affluence or well-being. Such affluent persons also suffer. They have no physical prop. When they interrupt their pursuit of possessions if only for a brief spell, they find an inner void, the specters of disappointment and meaninglessness before them. I believe that one perceives that even more painfully among young people and I should like to better things. But I don't know how. One closes oneself off to one's surroundings like an atom reactor, as it were, yet within one seethes and boils. I also note that the whole of life is like straggling along a mountain precipice—a sudden slippery fall, occasioned by alcohol and sexual experience, is possible every day at any moment.

Can the Church also hold "such young people." Surely not through beautiful ceremonies and prayer formulas or through a splendidly appointed church. Mystery-suffused sects are more interesting in this regard. They bring a change from the greyness of the everyday even though by so doing, they themselves would be bringing the greyness.

Please, dear Father Rahner, open an access to a Church that can give the person who enjoys material and physical well-being the same support it gives to the sick and the poor.

Many thanks for taking the trouble to reply,

Frank

Dear Frank,

You are a mathematics student. So I am assuming that you have a mentality that is very often come upon today in scientific circles. Given this mentality it is altogether possible to assert that such a scientist, as a result of a kind of occupational disease, to a certain extent suffers from a blind spot. In other words his rationality is somewhat hung up on what is directly experienced, on the notion that what is rational and subject to experiment can be mastered and understood. Obviously with such a mentality as a starting-point, it's not easy to find an approach to the mystery that governs our life, that we rightly and, at times, somewhat over-traditionally call God. You, for the very reason that you are a scientist will be so self-critical that for once you will have to reckon with the constrictions of your very intellectuality that your profession at once enjoins and entails.

It is indeed right to say that illness and indigence are situations in which a person can come to God. But only when he or she does this properly inasmuch as such situations can also provide a fertile soil for atheism. But to assert that such a situation is the only one in which a faith in God can develop would fare as a rather primitive opinion in the marketplace of ideas. The great thinkers of intellectual history, especially those of Greece and of the western world have grappled with the question of God in a positive sense, without being motivated by illness or poverty. And in my opinion your assertion that the Catholic Church understands and "masterfully so" how to transmit its faith to the poor and the sick and thereby serve as a prop to them can be faulted for also being a bit on the primitive side.

For, in the first place, it is we human beings who ourselves build this Church. And the notion that a Church preyingly, as it were, places itself alongside people and by employing a crafty and cunning tactic somehow and self-servingly brings them something of a supportive and consolatory value at times of distress or despair is a gross distortion of the real situation. I, for example, am one who longs for God and who, at the same time, is a member of the church as the community of these believers. And in my faith I do not feel myself as one being manipulated by a crafty Church outside myself.

You say that you do not belong to these poor and sick who need God, that you are a person of affluence, of well-being. I don't exactly understand what you mean by that. You yourself say that "such persons suffer." How come then that such persons are characterized only as "affluent," as those who enjoy "well-being?" You say that they have no physical prop. Do you perhaps mean psychic prop? The person who undergoes the experience of his or her inner emptiness, disappointment and the perception of the specter of meaninglessness in his or her life is still, nevertheless, a person who can find his or her way to God. Such a person must either be driven to despair by the absurdity of life or expediently (but, at bottom, culpably) escape into the banality of the everyday hustle and bustle with its tasks and pleasures.

In my opinion the reaction of such a person (and one that is ever right and responsible, to such a situation would be nothing else but the conviction of the reality of God himself. Now, of course, in a brief letter I cannot furnish any proof for the legitimacy of such a conviction of God's reality. The matter is hardly so simple. That you will after all eventually discern. And if now you want to flee, not because of indigence or illness, into a repeatedly contested faith in God, but for the purpose of arriving at such a conviction in a really responsible and life-shaping way, then you must also exact from yourself the effort required to seek for an answer to the God-question in present-day works of a philosophical and theological character within the Christian Church. I would not wish to recommend any particular work of this kind. But try the works of Hans Küng on this question or, if you can find nothing better, my *Foundations of Christian Faith, An Introduction to the Idea of Christianity.* Naturally, if you are able to make some use of such works you must study then thoroughly and patiently, with a certain effort, and also with a certain openness without the bias from the outset that you already know all and everything there is to know about the subject, and perhaps even better.

For the rest, a personal contact with the Church and with its life is altogether something that would be of significance to you in your present situation and therefore highly recommendable. The Church, after all, does not consist only of "beautiful ceremonies and prayer formulas." It, too, does not only want to bring a change from the greyness like the sects of which you write and which you find interesting. The Church is the community of those who in a lofty effort of their whole existence are embarked on a pilgrimage, believingly, hopefully and trustfully, toward the eternal mystery we call God, and who shape and structure their everyday life and their civic way of life on the basis of this ultimate attitude toward this mystery. The affluent, well-off person whom you describe and who is also a suffering soul in the face of the last questions of life likewise needs an approach to God and, in the final analysis, can find it only in a trustful co-existence with others who—in reference to Jesus Christ—try to accomplish this—their eternal life-mission.

Cordial greetings.

Karl Rahner

TWELVE

IT'S SO DIFFICULT FOR ME TO GO TO CHURCH

Dear Karl Rahner,

I am writing to you because I am convinced that you are rich in experience, open toward young people and approachable as regards their problems. I am studying educational theory and philosophy. My father is an academic and a religious man. I have six brothers and sisters. We are a bourgeois family in which "bourgeois" is viewed altogether in a positive sense by us. (I write this because most young people use this word as a metaphor for a so-called "philistine society," of which they take a very negative view).

Although I am the male heir of our family, I am never accorded preferential treatment, hence I am no "cock on the walk." As a result of this equality of all family members a strong harmony has crystallized among us children. The whole familial interaction is based on a very fundamental love. Since the day we were born my parents have worked and lived only for us children. My father's highest aim was always to raise us to be staunch Christians.

But he has not completely succeeded in this, his loftiest concern. However, before I go more closely into the religious problem, I should like to briefly describe my earlier years.

At an early age, as an altar boy, I joined the Catholic Youth Organization. At the same time I was a member of the Boy Scouts. At the age of ten our group broke up and from elementary school I passed on to high school. At 16 I was a young squad leader and one year later I also became a youth leader with the Young People's Red Cross. All these activities came to an abrupt halt when I turned 18, the year I took the examination to qualify me for university studies. After a brief second try I successfully passed the qualifying examination. I began my university studies one year later and joined a Catholic student association. Such is the brief history of my youth which surely moulded me into what I am today.

The problem, which has begun to concern me since the age of 17, relates to the religious sphere. I am a "convinced Christian" even though I believe that as such one must have at least some specialized theological knowledge. Although I lack this knowledge, I designate myself as a Christian, on the one hand because I have racked my brains over religions of the most varied kind, on the other, also because of my up-bringing.

A true Christian normally attends Sunday Mass. I almost never go to Mass! Often, I must confess, out of sheer laziness but much for the reason that the "Austrian Mass"—I live in Austria—is a "dead Mass." That perhaps may sound like a harsh judgment or prejudice so for the sake of clarification I shall describe what the so-called "living Mass" is for me. A Mass sung by blacks during which people clap their hands and shout as the Gospel is being sung . . . something very emotional and not only solidly rational. Such is the type of religious service that at times unfolds within my inmost imaginings. This type of religious service spreads life and hope and happiness, and I can draw strength from it.

I could willingly go often to such a religious service, and not only on Sundays. Unfortunately it exists only in my imagination when, at home, I lie in bed and reflect on things, perhaps also in an altogether doubting state of mind as I often have doubts concerning the existence of God. Nevertheless these doubts repeatedly vanish. You mustn't think, however, that I haven't also tried to find a content in our religious service. What am I to do if the religious service leaves me blank? It requires a great effort on my part to go to church. I would much rather prefer to be able to stand up, clap my hands (for example, in response to a stirring sermon) and sing out loud. But everything weighs me down, the stillness of the people, the singular mysticism that prevails in the church. All this stifles my inner commotion and brings my emotional flight toward happiness to nothing. The Mass proceeds like work on an assembly line. It's always the same, quiet and dead! To put it bluntly: "the Mass is routine!"

It would interest me to know whether the celebration of a Mass actually does not become a routine for you and a burdensome, prescribed obligation on your path. Can I, as a convinced Christian, instead of through the Mass also communicate with God in thoughts in my room, confess my problems and concerns to him? Were you a convinced Christian in your youth? Why did you decide to study theology? Do you ever entertain doubts concerning a real God, or is it only a "characteristic peculiar to our time" to doubt everything and to refuse to accept anything handed down from the past?

I would be very happy to receive a reply!
In Christian love of neighbor,

Bernard

Dear Bernard,

Forgive me if from the outset that I, in a necessarily brief letter, would not like to go deeply into the portrayal of your life up to now in your homeland, family and school, and that I also would prefer to refrain from answering the questions that you pose to me in the conclusion of your letter. I should like to limit myself to discussing your problem with the Sunday Mass.

You honestly admit that sometimes you miss Sunday Mass out of sheer laziness. Laziness ought to be overcome. But your problem is the "Austrian Mass," although the problem is probably the same in other countries of Europe. You say that for you the Mass is dead. Now I would first of all ask you whether you sufficiently make it a point actually to attend a religious service that at least creates less difficulties for you. After all religious services in our churches are still very different so, among the many that would be possibilities to explore, you should at least find one or the other that would be more acceptable and satisfying to you. You refer even to a "singular mysticism" that prevails in the church. Couldn't you wrest from that a more positive meaning? Just imagine if all the religious services every Sunday were to be like the one Church you describe in your letter. Would you gladly "stand up, clap your hands and sing out loud" every Sunday? Can you demand of your fellow-Christians, who also have their rights and their own mentality, that they attend such a service every Sunday?

To be sure there are Christians who attend religious services as a matter of routine. But what gives you the right to impute mere routine as the sole reason for Sunday attendance on the part of so many others? Is not also the performance of a religious practice as a "burdensome duty" perhaps an altogether authentic human performance and duty?

When you return to your family from the university (perhaps in a bad mood), isn't a gracious word to your parents or to your sisters, even if it doesn't come wholly from the heart, after all a meaningful obligation? Why shouldn't, in the same way, there also be an altogether meaningful participation in a religious service which does not especially stir your emotions at the first throw? Isn't the community with others, whom one may not immediately find likeable, perhaps something greater and more humane than the experience of a small like-minded group? Isn't the common celebration of the remembrance of the death and the resurrection of the Lord, which also has a decisive importance for your life, not more important and more glorious than any emotionality, perhaps a superficial one when all is said of it, to which you can give expression?

If you are simply swept off your feet by a frenzied piece of jazz music, is that a reason for refusing to listen to a rendition of Beethoven's Ninth Symphony instead of preparing yourself, at first perhaps laboriously, for an appreciation of such a human revelation? What I mean to say is that up to now you have never tried intensely and for long enough to find a meaningful content in the religious service, even if at times outer form may not be exactly conducive to such an appreciation and understanding.

You can, of course, as a convinced Christian,

pray in a quiet little room and ask God to forgive your sins and thus describe your problems to him. The Council of Trent recognizes a so-called spiritual conversion also outside the sacramental event and does not at all consider this a simple "as if" but as a true, grace-suffused event of union with Christ. But does that mean that everything, that ecclesial-ritual events in the community of the faithful are therefore meaningless or at least superfluous? You can lovingly just think of your parents and sisters and of the whole world to boot and that really signifies a reality of authentic community. But nevertheless you can, should and must cultivate a community with your family which brings all that which lives and should grow in the inmost core of your person into being a living community.

Inwardness, religious solitude and common religious celebration by no means signify a contradiction. Common religious activity is obviously subject to all the burdens and difficulties that such ritual events in the community bring in their train. Anyone who wants expediently to avoid these difficulties must ask himself or herself whether he or she, in the long run, celebrates the inner religious service of the heart in his or her life.

As for me (in order to touch on your closing question) it is obvious that, over the long run, one cannot avoid the naturally given danger of routine in the celebration of the Mass—or overcome this by abstaining from this celebration. By doing so a person no doubt avoids the danger of routine but, over the long run, one truncates the inner event in the heart, of which one is so proud. If I, who of course am not a moral theologian, were to be honest, I would admit that a quite conscientious and faithful Christian now and then can skip a Sunday Mass if by so doing he or she (unless excused from this obligation because of illness or something similar) in an honest self-criticism judges, without thereby simply succumbing to transient moods, that his or her disposition on this day is such that more is demanded from him or her of the Sunday Mass than he or she can give. Moralists may pronounce their judgment on my opinion and you must not take it as an excuse to simply yield to your love of comfort and to a certain underdevelopment in your religious capabilities.

Your life up to now after all has been the way it roughly ought to have been. See to it that this development proceeds further in the old direction and don't let this development run aground. When you have the opportunity—you were once an altar boy—try to actively participate in putting together a religious service that comes closer to what you quite rightly wish for.

With very cordial greetings,

Karl Rahner

THIRTEEN

BEAUTIFUL RESOLUTIONS, BUT
WHEN IT BECOMES TO ACTION . . .

Dear Father Rahner,

I am going to write you a letter on my own problems and cares. In order to give you a better opportunity to understand me, I shall first of all describe some fundamental situations in my life.

I am the son of religious parents. My father holds a rather high position. So I have been raised accordingly. I attended secondary school over which I was very happy and I was active in the Catholic youth group as well as an altar boy and group leader. When I became a neurotic and a depressive patient, my parents dispatched me to a closed off section of a clinic for nervous diseases where I spent the most horrible week of my life. At the base of all this were some previous suicide attempts and several outbreaks of depression. This stay in the clinic exempted me from military service. Instead I went to Israel for three months where I worked in a kibbutz. Since then I have been studying law . . . with little success. In the last semester I failed to pass the first state exam. Meanwhile I have joined a student association in which I feel very good. Certain characteristics have come to the fore, to a great extent because of my faults no doubt, which I do not know how to overcome, or whether such is even possible. My greatest worry is that I don't have either the will, the courage or the strength to overcome myself. I'm like a cork floating on water. I swim where the waves propel me and that despite the fact that I know it is not the right way. I find it infinitely difficult to stay at home evenings. So I spend them mostly at the student club or with friends, mostly playing cards, drinking or engaging in lengthy discussions.

To all this must still be added my laziness. I suspend all the eminently good resolutions that I had made to myself earlier when even their mere formulation had required some real effort. Often I resolved to give up smoking, but failed each time. I just can't sit down and study, I get ants in the pants sometimes even before they start crawling. The spirit is willing but the flesh is weak. I live according to this saying. After each disappointment I feel utterly worn out and depressed. Then I begin to drink and to dream of a better world. I have already fallen so low that on the following day I don't even feel out of sorts, I simply don't care, it's all the same to me. I have habituated myself to this rhythm. Each day begins and ends the same. I drink a lot and dream half through the day. A feeling of impotence has come over me. I would like to do something to counter my mistakes but I can't make allowance for the strain that it involves. So I'm slowly becoming useless.

And still I deceive myself because I would like to be somebody notwithstanding. Sometimes I imagine things that simply don't exist. And this goes so far that often I no longer know whether something really is or whether I am merely imagining it, wishing that it was really so. Perhaps there are also things in this letter that are not real, although I am trying to remain as objective and as critical as possible.

I feel best of all when I dream of a happy, safe and sound world. Often these dreams become romantic gushiness, a flight from reality.

Despite this romantic bent, as some call it, I lack any capacity for empathy with other people. When I was still in secondary school, I was the confidant of many of my schoolmates. They would come to me, unload their problems on me and I had to give them advice. After I had committed mistakes, such as leaking confidential information of the most different kind and also as the result of arrogant behavior, all the friends who had trusted me abruptly dropped me. It was a big shock to me and since then I have lost the capacity to empathize with another person—which I certainly once did possess. At times I ignore even the most primitive rules of civic co-existence, often I don't even recognize them. Ever since I lost the trust of those persons, I have had an exaggerated need for recognition. I try to be more than I really am. I would like to impress my friends and, at the same time, I disappoint them. Once I was scheduled to take an exam, and I pretended that I had already taken it although I had merely glanced at it. When my fellow club members learned about this, they demanded an explanation from me which I couldn't come up with (that evening I got drunk). I cannot show myself as I am. It would be too depressing. And I am also too cowardly for that.

Perhaps all this would be easier to overcome, if I weren't so strongly attached to my colleagues and friends. A good school colleague in the secondary school brought me to tears once when, as a joke, he ordered that I be sent home just to hurt my feelings. Perhaps I am too sensitive. I would like not to offend anybody and preserve what I have managed to build up. I am very attached to tradition.

I am often advised to set my life on another path, to look around for another place, to leave my friends, my studies, my present life behind. But I can't bring myself to give up my past because I'm afraid to lose contact with my friends.

Despite my sociable character, I find it difficult to show those who are close to me that I like them. The relationship with a girl that I once very gladly had broke up in the course of time because I couldn't trust myself to show her that I would attach a great importance to a closer friendship even though I knew that the inclination was not one-sided. I was afraid that I would have to give up a portion of freedom, a portion of my untouchableness—of my "Humphrey Bogartism."

When I come together with friends it is only seldom that I succeed in starting a serious conversation, in raising a ticklish theme. I can't stand out at evening gatherings where little is being said. If the others say little or nothing, I become the lone speaker and thus try to entertain everybody. It is only when I am alcoholized that I am able to earnestly talk with others. I am known as the alchy-philosopher. For this reason many do not take me seriously. So it goes, because I often entertain a whole circle, mostly through the sympathy of my fellows thanks to my boastful and bragging utterances and thanks to my incapacity to be serious in a crowd. I can't really get close to them.

In addition to all this I am not capable of being hard. An unpleasant feeling comes over each time I turn down someone who asks me for something. This is why I repair all kinds of utensils—I'm rather talented in these matters—I help here and there, although I should be doing something else that would be a further help to myself. I don't trust myself to ask for borrowed money back or to say no to anyone who asks me for a cigarette because I myself hardly have any money to buy them. Although I have a large circle of friends, I feel very much abandoned. I've become a loner because I've found no one, nor do I find the one to share my life with me and to take up the same struggle that I want to wage. I have lost the trust of most of my friends as the result of my drinking, and rather eccentric way of life. I lack the humility, the capacity to acknowledge mistakes. My fellow-creatures rightly despise my pride. Even back in the intermediate school my disputatious dogmatism made my teachers see red. It's easier to be humble and modest when one is successful and knows one's own talents than when one, as a result of one's own failure, looks for the feelings of success. And if they are not at hand, one tries to bring them into being with high-sounding talk.

All these problems and mistakes are reflected in my relationship to the Church. Earlier I was an enthusiastic altar boy, modest, ever ready to be helpful. At the age of 14 I spent two months in Ireland where I lived in a hostel in order to learn English. As the latter was conducted by the "Opus Dei," a lay order, there was much praying, and I was so enthused that I immediately wanted to join it, but a priest of the "Opus Dei" counseled me to wait a while longer. I participated in further "Opus Dei" events with the same enthusiasm as in Ireland. For example in a labor camp where we helped poor peasants with the field work or in Friuli, where we worked in the reconstruction of houses destroyed by the earthquake, and also in a ski-camp. I wanted even to become a priest, but I began to drink and to smoke and became increasingly weaker and lazier.

Today I no longer attend Sunday Mass, I go to confession only on great feast days and allow myself to succumb to expressions against God and the Church. Nevertheless I believe in him and pray now and then because I am convinced that there must be something that we call God. In my child-like faith I am always happy when during prayer I feel a shiver run down my spine because then I believe that God is inside me. To this day I still entertain the thought of becoming a priest, yet I still lack a sign from God that he needs me as his instrument. I am also lacking in many prerequisites for the vocation such as convictions, strength, industriousness, courage, etc. I am afraid to make such a decision probably also because of the obligation to observe celibacy.

Nevertheless I believe that whether I become a priest or not is unimportant. What I do consider important, on the other hand, is whether at the end of my life I can say that it was meaningful. At present I cannot in any case make such an assertion. The faith I now possess was transmitted to me by my parents and did not grow of itself in me. I fear the prospect that I might lose it as a result of my not wholly exemplary life because I already ask myself whether faith is altogether necessary. Now I live only from day to day awaiting a sign from God that will help me to escape this vicious circle, always preceded by repeated mendacious intentions to mend my ways by bouts of depression and inferiority complexes deadened by drinking and the intention to resolutely go toward my ruin.

Naturally I don't have only bad characteristics. I am also very musical, helpful, extroverted and am humorous and amusing when I'm in the right circle of friends.

I have already spoken with some persons on how to extricate myself from this morass. But most of the answers I have received have been unsatisfactory. Hence I would like to ask you, Father Rahner, as an eminent and experienced theologian, to tell me of your suggestions for resolving my problems.

With friendly greetings,

Matthew

Dear Matthew,

You are only 21 years old. It's hardly the end of the line. You can still make something of yourself. You did live quite reasonably and purposefully in the first 15 years of your life. You have had good experiences with others, and friends who trusted you. You were in Ireland and Israel and there have seen what one can accomplish. You have even participated in "Opus Dei" activities and noted that an intensive religious life in the service of God and of people can make one happy. Why shouldn't all these good experiences in your life not be proof that a new phase in your life can unfold in which you will overcome all that which, according to your own expressed feelings, is now so topsy-turvy in your life.

It goes without saying that your illness and your depressive disposition, which once brought you to a clinic for nervous diseases, are sure signs that you are also beset by difficulties for which you are not blameable. But even such difficulties can be weathered and overcome. You don't have to supinely give in to them. You once flunked an exam. So what?

An exam can be successfully taken again inasmuch as one has already learned something about the subject involved and with a little industriousness one can learn so much more about it and pass the second test with flying colors.

You often feel yourself in part through no fault of your own, often in part through your fault (that cannot be denied) in a state of weakness and despondency, by the feeling that you can't get yourself out of this vicious circle. There is first of all the danger that one secretly makes these weaknesses and depressive moods that no doubt exist, into a convenient excuse also to do nothing about remedying this situation whereas one can certainly do something about it. Therefore you should be self-critical against yourself. You can't really study all day long over your law books. But you can, at least, sit at your study desk a half-hour longer, say, than you would have actually wished or planned to do from the outset.

On your own admission you drink often and too much. You escape from depressive moods by resorting to drink. But you don't seem really to be an alcoholic properly so-called and therefore you must soberly and honestly tell yourself that you can no longer exculpate yourself when you go on a binge. One can control oneself, or can avoid occasions in which one drinks too much. You are under no obligation to play cards and to drink in your student lodgings. You can, if you really want to, impose a certain regulated way of life on yourself. If you are smoking and drinking too much because of your self-dissatisfaction—for which perhaps now and then you may have an objective ground—it is precisely in these situations that smoking and drinking are not to be viewed as the only possibilities, the only means for breaking out of such a mood.

I have the impression, given your obviously extravagant disposition, that you incline to extremes. Perhaps your situation, in the final analysis, stems from the fact that you wrongly demand too much from yourself, and when the high goal is not reached, you let yourself sink into states of depression from which all the things, which you very honestly and self-critically relate in your letter, subsequently ensue. Would it not be possible to cultivate a praiseworthy modesty, a rightly understood cult of a normal mean, a contentment with the average, and not to aspire to the highest so as not to fall into the pits?

The sober acceptance of life, as in most cases we must lead it, where shining hours and dazzling successes are rare, may perhaps do you lots of good. Furthermore: begin with some small, seemingly modest point of your life to demand something from yourself and actually to carry out what you perhaps find difficult to do.

You don't have to become a saint or what in your dreams you fancy it would be nice to be—in one stroke. But you can, at least once a day, smoke fewer cigarettes or even totally abstain from them for a few days or set aside a certain time for study. If you thus demand this or that from yourself and also really actualize them though they may seem trifling to you, you will note that you can even go further, that certain renunciations (somewhat solemnly stated) can also make one happy and prevent one from falling into pits of depression or from experiencing so-called frustrations of which there is so much talk in our day.

You note that I could actually say little in reply to your long letter. In contrast to your impressive self-portrait, my answer must strike you as pallid and run of the mill. Perhaps that stems from a lack in me of the requisite discernment and knowledge in appraising others. But perhaps it could also be an indication that at bottom, problematical as everything may seem, really not so much is lacking in you, that soberly and courageously this or that ought to be straightened out and be better organized in your life so that then the development that was planned in the first period of your life and that is far from being disavowed in these last few years, can really go forward.

I am convinced that something right and proper will come from you. Many personal histories are marked by periods such as you have gone through at the present time. It is far from necessary that such will be the leitmotif of your future life.

I think that we shall be seeing each other again soon and perhaps we can talk further. The main point, however, remains as I've already said: begin to effect perceptible individual accomplishments in your manner of life which as such may strike you as trifling but which, trifling as they may seem, bear within themselves the promise that your whole life will approximately become like the one that you picture in your dreams and that God wants from you.

Should you still wish to write a letter to me, you must also tell me what changes you have decided to put into practice.

Nowadays no one readily says this, one is easily embarassed and fears one's own grand words. Nevertheless I will dare say it: I am praying for you.

Cordially,

Karl Rahner

FOURTEEN

CONFESS—YES, BUT WHY TO A PRIEST?

Dear Karl Rahner,

"You, an altar boy, with a Christian upbringing, you stinking rich, you of all people have to steal!"

As a youngster I once had to listen to this sentence angrily passed on me along with a cannonade of further insults. But the charge is true. My friends and I, out of sheer boredom, had made a hobby of going into stores and shops and "ripping them off." On one occasion I was grabbed by the cops in a food store. I was sent home and I myself had to report the incident. My parents were deeply disappointed with me and ordered me to make my confession. I myself at that time felt like an heroic fighter and revolutionary against exploitation and capitalism. I went to confess a deed of which I was actually proud so as not to disappoint my parents once more. It struck me as a "tragicomedy" since I was confessing to something for which I, at rock bottom, felt not the slightest remorse.

This attitude, however, has been cultivated and instilled in us in our young years. We were forced by the school authorities to make two confessions every year. This unfolded roughly as follows. All us pupils were told that we were to go to confession on the next day. The teacher would lead us to the church. We all went inside. And one after the other we disappeared in the confessional. The confession, however, consisted only of a "hoarse whispering," of a memorized confessional formula and a litany of sins which had been heard earlier during the religious instruction period, such as for example, "I hit my sister," "I have spoken ill and disrespectfully of my parents," "I swore at the dentist . . . "

To be sure these faults and sins as well as similar transgressions characterize our life since we are but humans. Does it make any sense, however, to have to recite them in a hoarse whisper each time?

In the evening I very often try to reflect on my behavior and on my faults that marked the past day. Can I not confess directly to God inasmuch as I am conscious of my faults and regret having committed them and am also seeking for ways how to counter and reduce this negative behavior? And all this in a low-voiced conversation without indulging in loudly-spoken words in order to inform God of my sins and shortcomings and beg him for forgiveness.

Is it necessary to make one's confession to a priest? You have no faults, so perhaps you don't know what it's like to kneel in a confessional and confide the most intimate things to an unknown person. When I, for example, slept with a girl for the first time, I wanted to confess it since pre-marital sexual relations are prohibited by religion. I went to the church, entered the confessional and the moment my mouth opened it was only to suck in air and leave the booth. At the same moment I thought to myself: "God knows all about it anyway, so just what am I to confess?" Nevertheless I did tell him about it in a brief prayer. Is not confession often misused and violated as an alibi-establishing performance? I believe that in the course of technological development confession has lost the importance that it had in earlier, more mystical times. Humans have lost reverence on account of a great loss in emotionality. Intellect reigns, and when I view the problem of confession from the aspect of reason, I find it illogical to openly set forth my intimate life to a priest who has been made into a representative of God by the Church. For God, after all, sees all, and he is the only one who knows my inmost being. Given this standpoint, the aforementioned attitude, namely to speak alone with God in the stillness of a little room, would suffice. For anyone who is not a priest like yourself, lives very sinfully and in order to make an honest confession such a person would have to write down his or her sins everyday.

Try sometime to make a confession like a normal citizen in any confessional at hand! And if you should have as many faults as I, then you might perhaps get an idea of the problem.

I am hoping to receive a reply and send you many best wishes.

George

Dear George,

The question of confession, the sacrament of penance and its meaning is so complicated and stratified that if I were to write you about it, I could not even say something about pre-marital sex relations. And this is an even more difficult question. At all events you should also for once consider this question from another angle, namely by reflecting on what such an act may signify for the girl and her later life.

But let us stick to your question concerning confession. Obviously there is no sense in a mechanically and hoarsely whispered recital of one's sins in a confessional, and this is more than ever the case when one feels no remorse. The specific obligation to make a sacramental confession of sins, according to Church teaching, exists when on the basis of the matter involved and of a subjective discernment and freedom, a fault in the eyes of God exists, and one that essentially disturbs the actual, loving understanding of God. (Such, and only such, is a "mortal" sin which, according to Catholic tradition, will also be forgiven through God's word of forgiveness that we hear through the Church).

Hence it is quite obvious that impish hijinks, silly pranks, such as you relate at the beginning of your letter hardly fall in the category of faults requiring sacramental absolution through the word of the Church. Whether it can be meaningful to confess such "sins" is, once again, another question. At all events such a confession of transgression against God's commandments that do not objectively and subjectively and simultaneously signify mortal sins acquires a meaning only when the confessing person also really repents of this fault. I cannot say whether you, at the time that you engaged in this shop-lifting spree with your friends, were already in a position to really repent of such an act. But, in any case, you can now see that one doesn't wage a struggle against capitalism and exploitation and can't become a heroic fighter and revolutionary by such nonsensical histrionics.

You can see that such things are objectively

senseless, even though you could not subjectively discern it at that time. Nor is there any sense whatsoever in confessing one's sins in a hoarsely whispered and memorized confessional formula. Such comportment constitutes a perversion of the sacrament. I cannot, of course, write a treatise here and now on how a proper religious instruction and guidance to frequent confessions on the part of young people should be fashioned so that such a perversion of the practice of confession can be avoided . . . The practice that you have followed up to now, perhaps as the result of a religious and pedagogical bad practice on the part of the religious instructor, is of course sheer nonsense. But now you are a grown-up and you should try to gain an adult and Christian understanding of this sacrament.

It goes without saying that one can confess to God also outside the sacrament of penance those acts that in some greater or lesser way transgress against persons and against our relationship to God and his holy love. It is also Church teaching that when such a conversion occurs out of love of God, the forgiveness of the sin by God already begins. By that, however, the sacramental event of confession before a representative of the Church is not rendered meaningless. Rightly viewed, it is the way that corresponds to the nature of a human being and of a member of the Church wherein this interior conversion to God arrives at a consummation.

At the outset let me say again that it goes without saying that priests, too, are sinners and enjoined to confess their sins to the Church in the confessional. Hopefully they also do so. I believe that on the whole this frequency in the matter of sacramental penance is greater with priests than with so-called lay-persons. It

also astonishes me that you think such a confession of
the sinful Christian before the Church is meaningless.
Haven't you heard of the many people today who
manage to cope with their inner troubles and difficulties only when they try to make their inner
circumstances understandable to themselves and
overcome-able by recourse to a psychotherapist or a
depth-psychologist to whom they unburden themselves? Much nonsense, of course, can also transpire
on the couches of these psychologists. Hopefully you
will never have to take refuge with them for such
"disclosures" and do so, if ever, only if it's
psychologically and humanly necessary. But the ever
spreading practice of such psychic disclosures shows,
at least, that mortals in their normal state cannot so
sovereignly and self-glorifyingly cope with their inner
selves as you seemingly think you can, perhaps a bit
too overwhelmingly, as regards yourself.

Ask yourself sometime whether this authentic,
self-centered, conversion-minded confession, which
really corresponds to the earnestness and radicalness
of a fault in the eyes of God, occurs so often with
you, as you so remarkably presuppose in your
polemic against the sacrament of penance. I would
rather doubt that somewhat. If you in the midway of
your life, after the commission of a real mortal sin,
were to understand that this sin, in itself unabsolvable
by mortals, requires forgiveness from God, a
forgiveness that corresponds to the free love of God,
would you not also be intelligent enough to understand that one cannot in his or her life deal as blithely
with God, the holy, incomprehensible God, as all too
many fancy (on the basic and tacit assumption that
what has to them become something enveloped in the
mists of time past, also no longer exists in the eyes of

God), and you would intuitively have grasped that it is a wonderful thing to experience something akin to what befell the sinners of the Gospel, those sinners to whom Jesus says: your sins are forgiven. Whereby the on-lookers, astounded and shaken, asked: "Who can forgive sins but God?" None indeed but the God whose forgiveness is not accorded in the matter of course way and as cheaply as you seem to presuppose, accompanied, moreover (excuse me for being so blunt) by an airy, smug self-satisfaction even there where you admit that you have sinned.

Bear in mind for once, furthermore, that actually all faults, however hidden they may seem to be in the inmost recesses of the heart, are also faults against our neighbor. This applies even more to the sins that directly and palpably violate the commandment that enjoins the love of neighbor, that indeed is quite manifest with most sins. But, at bottom, it also applies to such sins that seem to belong solely to the sphere of a private inwardness. Evil thoughts, unrestrained egoism, wicked pride and all such things (Jesus has stressed that) ultimately affect and influence the behavior of a human being in his or her relationship to others. When one sees the social dimension of one's sin—if we may so put it—and takes it seriously, one should also understand that one's sin is also directed against the holy community of the Church. It therefore follows that a forgiving word of the Church, of the holy community of the people of God, is also meaningful and important. Vatican Council II has expressly stated that in the sacrament of penance the fault of human beings against God and the Church are jointly forgiven.

You young people of today are always asserting that you have a deeper and more radical understanding of society, of a political theology, of social criticism, of the tasks of the international community, than we individualists of a time past.

I think it wouldn't hurt if you would also become a little like religious socialists (rightly understood) in regard to the sacrament of penance.

I have not by a long shot said everything concerning the Church's sacrament of penance, about its importance and position in the religious experience of a real Christian. But if you begin with the hints that I have given and if you also, through further life experience, more clearly make your own the seriousness of the life of a human being before God and his holiness, then, I think you can also gain a more positive and living relationship to the sacrament of penance—a relationship that will transcend all your bad boyhood experiences with the gift of the paschal Jesus to his Church.

With all good wishes,

Karl Rahner

FIFTEEN

I NEVER HAD ANY GUILTY FEELINGS
AFTERWARDS

Dear Father Rahner,

I am studying theology and I very soon am scheduled to take the final examination. Later I should like to enter the teaching and pastoral profession. I have received a religious education, my father was very involved in ecclesial affairs. At the age of seven I became an altar boy and since then I have been a member of various youth groups, always in contact with some open-minded priests. Thus my life has been stamped by religious persons and personal experiences with an ecclesial background.

And therein lies my problem: at fifteen I made the acquaintance of my first girl friend. We were barely eighteen when we slept together. The relationship which was very close fell apart when we became twenty-one because our conception of life and ways of life were too different.

Then I made the acquaintance of two other girls with whom I also had a sexual contact. I met my present wife two and a half years ago, and we have been engaged for a year. My wife became pregnant during our period of engagement and we got married (which we had planned to do later anyway). We are very happy with each other and very happy over our child.

I have never had any guilt feelings despite my awareness of my many inconsiderate acts and I did not shrink from an honest confrontation in the confessional booth.

I should like to ask: does all this signify a vanishing morality? Or is a radical change in the making which the Church (the official one) is still lagging behind?

How do you view the problem of pre-marital sex and also of extra-marital sexual relationships when the inclination is very powerful—perhaps only for the reason that a marriage cannot be consummated due to external circumstances. Can the only answer to the long period of time between puberty and the material and educational preconditions that make a marriage a possibility be the injunction to practice "ascetisism," precisely in those cases where the relationship is of a deep kind, as was the case formerly when, given the shorter educational period, a marriage would have been viewed and contracted as a matter of course? What questions must an unmarried couple pose to themselves when they want to express their relationship also in a physical way?

I'm not alone with this problem—many friends of mine act similarly or find too little help for them to be able to orientate themselves.

Please point out some orientational possibilities to us!

Cordial greetings,

David

Dear David,
You have, as one notes in your letter, studied theology well. Thus it is relatively easy for you to

summarize all the questions that today concern and afflict a Christian in regard to sexual morality almost on a brief page. But, hopefully, you will also understand that one cannot answer in as brief a manner as you request. Therefore I shall decline even to make the effort to answer these questions and, at the same time (which would be necessary) attempt to do justice to both the psychological and social situation of our time as well as to the traditional teaching of the Church. As a result, of course, one need neither bemoan the vanishing morality among young people nor posit, reluctantly, a radical change in Church teaching the frontiers of which, even as regards where they ought to be drawn, are also beyond anyone's ken.

Allow me only (I can't and won't do anything more here) to ask some questions. It astonishes me that in respect to your former life in this area you apodictically assert: "I have never had any guilt feelings." Where, then, actually exists the "honest confrontation" (with yourself, with your life) that, according to your word, you did not shrink from in the confessional? Have you sufficiently pondered the fate that has befallen your former girl friends as a consequence of your common experiences for which you are responsible? Have things in their lives also proceeded so simply without experiencing severe shock and deep human wounds, as you seem unquestioningly to assume? I'm glad that you are now living in a state of happy marriage. But can you simply dismiss, in every respect, as harmless your relationship to your present wife in the two and a half years before your marriage? You must certainly realize that this "period of engagement," owing to the lack of total commitment (an omission which also obtained with your previous girl friends) might have turned out quite differently even for your now—thanks be to God—beloved and sincerely esteemed wife?

Was, then this relationship to your wife before your marriage really as "deep" as you say inasmuch as you come on, as it were, with a casual, dismissive and unabashed air in regard to your previous girl friends. Was your relationship to those other girls also so "deep?" If yes, then you should not recall your relationship with them . . . as calmly and self-assuredly as you do. If so, how could you have so blithely entered into so intimate a relation with them, as "sleeping-together" at the age of 18, after all, is? Have you not in your present relationship also already had experiences that actually should lead you to reflect once more and with greater earnestness on your earlier life and thus arrive at the realization that the traditional sexual morality enjoined and espoused by the Church cannot be annulled with an instantly postulated "radical change?"

I am aware, of course, that I am far from having provided a really sufficient answer to the many questions posed in your letter. But you, after all, are a theologian of sorts, you can read theological books and, after all, beyond a mildewed and old-fashioned moral theology of yore there are earnest theologians and earnest and honest books on these questions. Come to terms with them. Examine what is contained in them. Examine your own life, then through study and further life experience a complex of the norms of sexual life will surely occur to you, and along with an upright acceptance of what is today really binding in the Church's teaching on marriage. These new awarenesses will help you get on in your own life, in your work with young people as well as in your approach to the problems of our time.

I regret that I cannot write more. But you are clever and gracious enough to perceive the impossibility of continuing further in such a brief letter.

All best wishes for you, your marriage, your Church and your work.

Karl Rahner

SIXTEEN

TWO POSSIBILITIES FOR GIVING
A MEANING TO LIFE

Dear Professor Rahner,

Of late I have been intensely concerned with questions concerning the meaning of life. For this reason I would very much like to hear an opinion on this matter from an experienced adult and, moreover, from a representative of the clergy.

I have advanced the following theory: the life of a microbe surely has no meaning for it. However, it altogether has a meaning for organisms at a higher stage of development, perhaps for human beings, whatever the meaning may be in a special case. One can rationally consider this fact as a link in an infinite and temporally unlimited series from which it can be concluded that each phenomenal form of life has an objective meaning only if viewed from a higher stage—whereby, for example, all humankind would be viewed as a link in this infinite system.

Hence, in my opinion, only two possibilities are proposable to the individual for the purpose of giving an objective meaning to life (there are, of course, many subjective meanings as, for example, nicotine, alcohol, money, work). A first possibility would be to achieve, or to do something in one system that has an eternal existence. For example, fame won as the result of a history-making feat.

The second, perhaps easier possibility, would consist in the belief that we are indeed a subordinate part of a system. However, with the end of earthly existence this state likewise ends and a state outside the dimensionally narrow limited systems ensues which then stands forth as the objective meaning. This road no doubt is risk-ridden to a greater degree, yet it can be traversed more comfortably. Nevertheless I have opted for it and am now looking for some rational or theological arguments to buttress this theory.

Thank you in advance for the trouble you will be taking.

Charles

Dear Charles,

I find it interesting to note how you are already beginning to philosophize in your young years. Most of your chronological peers are much too comfort-loving to wrestle with such questions. Of course, in your philosophy in which you try to allot a definite place in a "system" to each existent, you must also consider that the human being is simply not only a single, subordinate portion of a higher over-all system. Rather, in the final analysis, through his or her very knowledge of the system itself the human being once more has a wholly different relationship to the whole of reality—a relationship at all events that is quite different from that peculiar to a part that is only a part of the system and knows nothing whatsoever of the whole. Hence it also has no free and responsible attitude to the whole. What's more, the human being—insofar as he or she has or ought to have a knowing and loving relationship to the primary ground of all reality—to the primary ground that we call God, can and must once more pose and answer the "question of meaning" in a wholly different way than those realities of the world system which from the beginning—even in their limited reality—are also comprised in the sub-human sphere.

To be sure the real meaning for human beings is not to be sought in nicotine, alcohol, money, work. Neither, however, must it be sought in fame and in a history-making feat since, at bottom, all these things are transient and have no "eternal existence." The ultimate, true and final meaning for a human being lies at the base of his or her openness in mind and in freedom to the totality of all reality and its divine primary ground that—as we know at least through the Christian revelation—wants to communicate to us human beings precisely this infinite meaningful primary ground—ultimately understandable only in itself—that we call the direct intuition and contemplation of God.

I think that if you take seriously the theory of your life, alluded to at the end of your letter, and also think it out to the end, you can achieve a real understanding for the interpretation of the total reality of human life that the Christian faith offers us.

Cordial greetings,

Karl Rahner

SEVENTEEN

IS TRUST IN GOD ENOUGH?

Dear Father Rahner,

My question: what is more important, love or the gift of a vocation and can the one replace the other?

I am 19 years old and for several months I have been attending the specialized college for religious pedagogy with the aim of becoming a religion teacher. I made this decision suddenly after I had given up the notion of taking a training course in another field. At first I was totally at sea for two months. Then in the space of two weeks I decided on a course in religious instruction. But I have been assailed by doubts since the end of November and I ask myself whether being a religious teacher is the right vocation for me. I repeatedly try to repress this question, as it is altogether my habit to do whenever I'm in a quandary. But now I have firmly resolved to come to a decision by Easter. This is why I would be very pleased to receive your counsel.

Why do I doubt that this vocation is the right one for me? I would describe myself as a rather composed and contact-poor person. At all events it is hard for me to express my thoughts in words and express what I would like to say (especially when talking). People who know me pretty well know what I mean when I say something but I could certainly never communicate the essentials of our faith to children. (I would, above all, like to teach in an elementary school.)

A second reason is that I am afraid of ending up teaching in a routinized, listless manner. As a full-time religion teacher I would have to teach 24 hours a week. That may not sound like a lot but it comes to 12 classes and from time to time three so-called parallel classes. That means that I must always teach the same subject in the classes, although the hours can be arranged differently.

Isn't one's teaching bound to become mechanical and spiritless in such a situation? Can one manage to be as lively and exciting in telling stories on the third time around? I am convinced that one cannot. I believe that I won't be able to, in spite of all my love for the children and the profession. I know the song "always to trust in God . . . " Is that enough? And the longing to communicate to children God's love for us mortals? Unfortunately I do not have any other prerequisites.

I am glad to have been allowed to write you this letter, and that I was forced to formulate all that which for a long time has lain on my heart.

Cordial thanks,

Gabriel

Dear Gabriel,

It is natural that the profession to which you have been aspiring for some time should entail difficulties for your giftedness. Twenty four hours of religious instruction are no small thing. I know that the danger of a spiritless routine must always be overcome anew. But it seems to me that I can read an earnest faith from your letter. You write indeed that you have a longing "to communicate to children God's love for us mortals." With this, actually, the decisive prerequisites for your profession already exist and all the other difficulties, which I will not try to minimize, are after all overcome-able. Why shouldn't you learn to say to children what you inwardly feel? You were, as I hear, a youth group leader. You certainly must have had the experience that you can get along with young people and your "contact-poverty" is not as bad as you assess it. Calm, modesty, and similar character traits that you deem to be difficulties for this profession can altogether be employed in a positive sense and direction.

Naturally I don't know whether you (you are barely twenty) will be encountering other experiences that you have not had up to now and then perhaps a change in your plans may occur. You can serenely reckon with such a possibility, but also composedly await, trusting in God and his guidance of which you yourself write.

With best wishes and cordial greetings,

Karl Rahner

EIGHTEEN

LIFE IS UNBEARABLE WITHOUT ILLUSIONS

Dear Father Rahner,

I have many questions and find no answers. In the final analysis I must probably myself find answers by following my conscience. But I need someone who extends me a helping hand.

Sometimes I fancy that I can build my own ideology. I want to be happy without harming others. This sounds very simple and the whole problem, say, of pre-marital sexual relations would be settled. Sometimes I frantically persuade myself that I—when I sleep with and am tender with someone—can after all only be doing good. At bottom, however, all that never really begets the fulfillment of which there is always so much talk.

I am afraid of reality and I am manipulable. I know that one must work hard at it everyday by oneself in order to sustain belief in God—but I shrink from such a task. Besides I am afraid of imperative demands enjoining chastity, unselfishness, discipline, loyalty, readiness to make sacrifices, not to be "pushy" and many others. Sometimes when I feel like generating a little joy I turn my casette recorder on—then I'm happy for a few minutes and to some extent feel a psychic balance. But soon it's all the same as before.

It means, no doubt, all such castles in the air are dangerous because one then can no longer separate illusion from reality. But I'm afraid that I simply cannot endure reality without illusion. I am afraid of reality. In my book reality is not doing your homework, scolding teachers, almost daily sermons from my mother. I am afraid of being a failure in every respect and of losing friends in consequence of my failure. Must I, after all, assume that human failure is only to be made up for through God? I suspect that I can reconcile myself with myself only with God's help.

But I cannot rightly reconcile myself with the Church. When I think "Church" I associate it with "chastity" which I feel is an inhumanness that even rejects self-gratification. Of course I don't know whether I derive the word inhumanness from the word human being as God created and willed him or her. What actually constitutes the "true" human being? I clearly perceive that I still have a long way to go in order to reach God. But I will try to go to him. The more I think upon it, all the more do I make the demand on myself to know the "truth" (which presumably I will never be able to grasp).

There still clings to the Church, and all too much so, what strikes humans as negative. The Church proposes renunciation, sacrifice, self-discipline, etc. as behavioural models, yet it cannot plausibly and persuasively explain that these qualities are really sources of joy for human beings: despite my scepticism I am now, as before, convinced that the ideas of the Church are good, that I can find God only through them. But how am I to find these values, if they lie buried under prejudices, bad explanations, bad examples, smugness, love of one's own comfort and self-glorification.

Dear Father Rahner, I of course do not await an answer to all these questions. I hope only (and very much so!) that you out of your extensive sacerdotal experience can bring a little light to my total darkness.

I thank you for your trouble.

Christine

Dear Christine,

I write you with a bad conscience since I let this letter lie around unanswered for all too long. Meanwhile much in your life has changed. You have a child. This child is your child. You have thereby brought into being a personal history in the making and you are responsible (co-responsible) for it. It is a personal history that will nevermore end. But one that finds an eternal final destiny before God.

A life, such as is now yours, effects many changes. This is why I cannot really say very much in reply to your letter. Read it yourself once more and ask yourself whether the statements contained in it, if one ponders over them scrupulously, do not contradict each other and whether this contradiction may not be nothing else but the echo of contradictions that you must iron out in your life. When you gaze at your child, you are also gazing on your indescribable life-responsibility, but also on a reality before which you, in the final analysis, have no fear. Rather, you love it and therefore you embrace this responsibility. At this point in your life imperatives enjoining unselfishness, loyalty, readiness for sacrifice and a modest unassertiveness and many others, becomes understandable and acceptable to you. Here after all you note that only there can real happiness be achieved and not, say, by turning on your casette recorder, fancying thereby that you can achieve a psychic balance in such an easy way.

If at this point in your life you simply let fear be fear, hold the fort day after day and soberly bear the duty that every day brings, you need have no fear of becoming a failure and of losing real friends who are worthy of the name. Then you must also confidently reckon that human failure is after all judged by God—by the God of whom one ultimately knows something perhaps when one lets one's failure be forgiven and does not hermetically withdraw into one's self and think that this failure is the last word in his or her life and of reality in general.

I would prefer not to write on your relationship to the Church. Give the Church the chance to gradually become more understandable to you through self-critical experiences that you have with yourself as your life moves on. After all you yourself say that you, despite your scepticism, are convinced that the ideas of the Church are good and "that I can find God only through them." Indeed you note that much about the Church that displeases you perhaps springs from "prejudices, bad explanations, bad examples, smugness and love of one's own comfort and self-glorification." In the final analysis it is not actually a matter of the "ideas" that the Church preaches, but of the experience that one can learn if one has good will. We are all Church in loving community, Church, which despite all disappointments gives us trust in a final blessed denouement of our lives, which finally is promised to us not through remarkable ideas, but through the life of Jesus, of the Crucified and Resurrected One.

I don't think that you are in "total darkness" at all, but you can serenely, courageously and trustfully embrace the "glimmer of light" that now beams in your life—thanks be to God, without me—perhaps directly from the face of your child.

Most cordially,

Karl Rahner

NINETEEN

BIDDING FAREWELL OVER AND OVER AGAIN

Dear Father Rahner,

I am the carpenter who at our meeting presented himself to you for a few moments. I am not writing you just for the sake of posing a question to a distinguished professor, but in order to receive from him a practical answer. I write you therefore because I as a tree expect from you deep soil and a better and more vigorous growth.

Farewell, just what is that? Of late I have become conscious of so many moments and variations of farewells, that I can barely distinguish between separation or farewell, reunion or farewell, disappointment or farewell, beginning or farewell, death or farewell.

Is it a farewell when a friend of mine is hopelessly surrendered to the control of drugs?

Is it a farewell when two work-mates and friends of mine suddenly die?

Is it a farewell when I for two long years invest love, sorrow, pictures, letters and patience in a girl and suddenly no longer feel a need for this girl?

Is it a farewell when I die?

When I die, will my weaknesses also continue to

live alongside my virtues?

What is the difference between farewells as hope and farewell as surrender?

When one has grown used to another person, is the farewell in this case the same as giving up smoking?

When one loves another person—can one take one's leave from this person the way Abraham did with his own son?

One thing, however, is sure: I experience each farewell very keenly. Nevertheless I don't know what I should learn from them, what conclusions I should draw.

Thanks,

Clement

Dear Clement,

We know each other, of course: you are the carpenter and I hope that you soon pass your apprentice examination. I am not at all the deep soil from which the tree of your life can find a better and more vigorous growth. Nevertheless I will try to write a few sentences on your question. You ask what a farewell is actually supposed to be.

Now, as you yourself have noted, there are different kinds of farewell and mentally one cannot easily subsume them under one heading. Certainly, one attribute that belongs to the notion of farewell in a real sense is the inner relationship that one had to the person from whom (or to the situation from which) one must take leave or bid farewell. One cannot speak of a real farewell when indifferent persons or fully indifferent realities take their leave. But when it involves persons or matters that have had a real importance, then one can properly speak of farewell. One can also take leave of oneself.

For at the moment of death, at least, each one in a certain sense takes leave from oneself, from one's free self-regulation and from one's life as an accomplished or even unaccomplished task and must abandon oneself wholly to God. But this is certainly a farewell that one cannot easily compare with others.

In my opinion one must make essential distinctions in the matter of farewells, namely, whether one is taking leave of another person or another reality culpably or non-culpably. Whoever breaks a bond of loyalty, whoever lets another depart to whom he or she really owes his or her attention, his or her love, really is making a bad farewell. Whoever perverts, slanders an authentic experience of his or her life, to which he or she should have clung and does not preserve it in the remembrance that belongs to his or her personal history, also makes a culpable farewell. The question that then naturally rises is: can amends for this fault be made forthwith, can one return to the culpably forsaken person or experience? That will be different in individual cases. A final forgiveness of such a fault, if one can no longer go back to the abandoned person or to the lost experience, is certainly always possible through God's grace. But the recovery from such a loss in which what has been lost comes back to one from God in an incomprehensible way in any case is something that can be attained only through a real petition for forgiveness, through genuine remorse, through a real endurance of the pain over the loss. There is certainly no room here for frivolousness, sluggish thinking and cheap repression of guilt feelings.

Conversely, however, there are also farewells

that have nothing of a culpable character about them. Rather, they are even a task and a duty assigned by life itself. Scripture recognizes and sanctions that a child must leave father and mother. Even such a farewell may perhaps be accompanied by grief and perhaps place one before the experience of loneliness and insecurity. But it is a farewell that must be because a human being must become independent and self-reliant and assume responsibility for his or her own life.

There are many such and similar farewells. St. Paul speaks of putting the things of childhood behind him. We will always and over and over again be taking leave from much that has become dear to us and that seemingly had safely belonged to our life. Actually every night we bid farewell to the day that has been granted to us at dawn. We must learn to give up this and that, what once signified joy or a gratification to us because we recognize that we must give them up for the sake of a higher, richer, more fulfilled life. Thus there are leavetakings from persons who are really close to us. The missionary who sets out for far-off foreign lands must leave much behind that was dear to him or to her.

Those who marry in a way step out of the circle of their former friends and must concentrate their lives in a manner different from before, on the marriage partner. And those who really apply themselves to a profession and want to achieve something in it, of necessity must bid farewell to some pleasures and some activities to which they had pleasurably dedicated themselves in younger years. It can almost be said that one can only live and mature and can lead a real life that is worth living when one has learned how to take one's leave.

The direction that farewells or leave-takings should take is a matter that differs from case to case. I cannot now give you a recipe that covers them all. You say at the end that you often weep when a leave-taking becomes unavoidable. One can nearly say: learn to weep and take off, nevertheless! Learn to bid farewell without looking back.

You surely must know the biblical story of Lot's wife who was turned into a pillar of salt when during her flight she stopped to turn around to look at her homeland as if happiness and life were to be found only there. Learn not to look backward but forward in the confident conviction that even after a farewell—that is fate or duty—the real, whole and blessed good still lies before you.

I wish for you that you will soon pass your apprentice examination with great success. This also will be a farewell because you will be called upon to fulfill new, hitherto unexperienced duties. Don't look back, go forward!

I wish you all the best.

Karl Rahner

TWENTY

I ALMOST NEVER THINK ABOUT GOD

I come from a background of easy, ordered circumstances, I have sunny disposition and take joy in
life. At first sight everything with me is in order.
Nevertheless I often face questions and problems that
make me feel insecure. In most cases the solution to
these problems comes with time, and this is a source
of satisfaction to me. But in the last few years one
question has persistently plagued me to which I cannot give a sure answer.

On the one hand I believe in God and I accept the
idea of an eternal life after death, on the other, my
life-situation is a very comfortable one. I like to enjoy
myself and later would like to embark on a career and
earn money. When such matters are involved I am
very ambitious. And to a sufficient degree I have the
requisite resoluteness. I am very active but sometimes
have the impression that I live carelessly without giving my life a greater guiding principle or a deeper
meaning. Sometimes I don't even have the strength to
go to church or to say a short prayer. In this regard I
am indeed very cautious. When I reflect on how much
time I devote to thinking about God I come to the
conclusion that it amounts to almost nothing.

Therefore I would like to ask you whether it suffices to believe only in God and, all things considered, to lead an honest life in which actually God never occupies the first place? Or should one have an active sense of God—with the Church—so as to avoid an "unpleasant surprise" when one appears before God?

I have often discussed that question with friends of my own age but no one knew how one draws an exact line between a good and bad, a wasted and fulfilled life, in other words, "between heaven and hell."

I hope that I was able to make myself understandable and I hope you can reply.

Cordial thanks in advance.

John

Dear John,

You describe your situation very clearly in your letter and actually I think that it is the situation of every human being between heaven and earth, between God and the world. We have a commandment that enjoins us to love God with all our heart and undividedly, and you also perceive the urgency and difficulty of this commandment. But we are human beings between world and God. As concerns the undividedness of a radical love of God, we are still "on the way." But we must also be aware of this and reckon it in our manner of life.

To proceed first of all to the other end of our problem, I would like to say: You may serenely go about being ambitious, wanting to pursue a career, and earn money. In your phase of life and in your concrete situation such a determination does not need to be positively inspired by the love of God. God does not at all demand that of you, at least not yet. Hence worldly motivations that determine life are not bad because they do not come from God, from the heart's core, where God communicates himself to us and wants to be loved, in a tangible and experiential way.

But nevertheless even in this situation of becoming, of beginning one can, and not merely abstractly, believe in God, but also try to love him. One can pray, one can also, beyond his or her own legitimate, ambitious plans and strivings, live and work, assume responsibility and work selflessly for others in a "community" of the most different kinds (the family, the church, a youth group, etc.). The whole greatness of such a life is, of course, something indefinable, an unsystematic blend of the heavenly and the earthly that is not so exactly perceptible and definable, that ever remains something improvised. But once more your task is to patiently accept precisely this mixture with confidence and with trust in God.

You ask, and in the final analysis, I believe that the answer can be only the encouragement to endure your question patiently and trustfully. I cannot recommend that you already become only a heavenly human being burning with love of God with no other motivations. But even much less still can I say, "Perish, absorbed in the earthly, only in your active disposition." You will not be able to avoid being a creature of this earth and a child of God at one and the same time. You can and should be both and trust that the final reckoning of your life balances out even if you cannot exactly verify or determine whether everything balances correctly in this final accounting.

Cordially,

Karl Rahner

TWENTY-ONE

CALLED INTO LIFE IN ORDER TO COME UNDER DEATH'S CONTROL

Dear Father Rahner,

I am very glad to be allowed to write to you because I am wrestling with a problem that only an expert like yourself can solve.

I do not believe in God. This is not just a phrase that so many young people are always mouthing. I have pondered over the question and I believe that it would be better not to believe in God because otherwise one would also have to accept the notion that he is a sadist and a misanthrope. I came to this conclusion when I reflected on things and clearly recognized the fact that there is much misery, deceit, murder and other evils in our world. If God were our good father, he certainly would not allow that. For no father, were he of the worst kind imaginable, would hurl his children into misery. Nevertheless I would better understand such an earthly father who would do such a thing more than I would God. For the Church, after all, teaches us that God is almighty. An earthly father, however, surely is not. God has the absolute power, he, according to the Roman Catholic faith, as well as according to the faith of other religions, created us and also is well-intentioned towards us. And if he knows everything, then at the moment of our creation he must have also known how we would develop.

In the Bible there is a passage describing the destruction of Sodom and Gomorrah. These people who lived there had also sinned against God and were punished with death. Is God therefore also planning our annihilation? Did he create us only in order to destroy us? Unfortunately, I see no logic in this and in any case no goodness.

Perhaps we have also escaped God's power since there are so many murderers who have violated one of the most important of God's commandments and who run about unpunished! Can he no longer pronounce judgment, has he no longer power over us? Has what happened to Frankenstein happened to him in that his creation has grown taller than he?

You can see then that my views do not coincide with those of the Church. I would be very pleased to receive an answer to my questions from you.

Cordial thanks in advance,

Robert

Dear Robert,

First of all I am surprised that you openly participate in the activities of the Catholic Youth Group although you declare yourself to be a convinced atheist. Perhaps there is still something else afoot, among your would-be atheist reflections. At least the question as to whether something like God exists.

You will realize, of course, in a brief letter I cannot answer and master the whole question that you bring up in a few pages.

Nevertheless I would like to say that it also occurs to me that the question concerning the suffering in the world, concerning the terrible misery and woe in the world—wrought by nature or human beings—can lead to an atheism. Such a view born of reflection on the inexplicable suffering in the world is the only atheism that seriously gives me food for thought. Someone once said that after Auschwitz no one could any longer believe in God. I don't consider this assertion correct. Yet it is an earnest utterance born of the despair over all the horrors that occur in the world.

But then first of all I ask myself: "Does all this become more endurable, better, easier to cope with if one is an atheist? Or is such a position the recognition of a final determination, of all this terror and fear rampant in the world? Must not one precisely then, when one feels solidarity with the gassed, with the napalm-burned children, with the inmates of concentration camps, etc.—must one not precisely then, even if with a last exertion of mind and heart—demand that there *be* that infiniteness of strength, of power, of love, in which all that is once more meaningfully and blessedly annulled?

Things, of course, are not such that we could formulate a positive conception of God and, on that basis, let all that in the world that terrifies us to our bottommost depths and tries to drive us to despair dissolve like a harmless delusion. Things, of course, are just not that way. But nevertheless I would like to ask you, who appeal to logic and sober reflection, whether you may not have a short-circuited and all too primitive conception of God on the basis of which, of course, the suffering in this world constitutes an absolute contradiction.

If God is much greater than suffering which

ultimately is finite, then it is still incomprehensible how this suffering can co-exist with God. At all events, however, it is not a contradiction that an infinite good God can permit this suffering because he precisely in his—albeit incomprehensible to us—plenitude of life, meaning and being can really make this suffering in the world meaningful and can also annul it.

The actually prevailing situation is such that the atheist, for whom this suffering has an absolutely, unresolvable conclusiveness, must explain this suffering as a phenomenon that ultimately is of no consequence, as finite, as an inevitability of a developing nature ever dissolving itself anew in its forms in an eternal recurrence. The atheist has the least right to take this suffering in the world with especial seriousness. Suffering is a true problem only for a person who believes that God exists as a holy, just, loving, infinite mighty God. He does not then solve or surmount it but he can really perceive that on the basis of his position he can take this suffering more seriously as a question than an atheist who, at bottom, must needs be satisfied with the absurdity of this world, of this evolution of nature, of this eternally recurring rise and fall.

You must not conceive of a God who assertedly is powerless vis-a-vis suffering. Were you to think that, you would have a false conception of God. You do not have to assert that you understand how God and suffering could co-exist, and reciprocally would not call each other into question. But you should not assert that the God, who is the real God, and who is thus above all your human concepts of him and infinitely above all your demands on him, could not cope with this suffering.

Marxists have already often ridiculed the Christian faith as an opiate for those who are short-changed through the suffering in this world. But I ask you, have you a better answer for these poor, for those who are short-changed, for these starving and dying, and lastly also for yourself? You can derisively say that Christians would console themselves with the hope of a future heaven because this world is unendurable. Yet I presume that you will say that so long as things are still going tolerably well with you. I believe that the question of God, viewed in terms of suffering in the way that you do can be espoused only by those who can afford the luxury of making an intellectual problem out of suffering. The ones who really suffer in the extreme, who must either radically despair or always assert that their suffering is not all that bad, that death is the most normal thing that is altogether conceivable, or they will believe in God and the incomprehensibleness in which alone their really bitter question up to the end is once more annulled. And, indeed, in the final analysis also and only through the unconditioned love of this incomprehensible God.

You interpret your experiences of suffering as an argument against God. Have you even once tried to make of your experiences of happiness, of meaning, of joy, of shelteredness likewise into an argument from which the presentiment of the eternal God of light and blessedness can unfold in you? Or do you experience suffering as a stimulus to an absolute protest, and the good of this world as something banal and to be taken for granted? Are you really so correct and objective in regard to the ambivalence of your experiences? Think upon this further, do not absolutize the bitternesses of your own life. A little light is enormously more than a darkness that seems to be without end.

I don't have the impression that my letter, that has necessarily turned out to be brief, is especially remarkable or helpful. But perhaps it will challenge you to be cautious and not to consider your own argumentation so penetratingly perceptive, so telling and irrefutable.

With cordial greetings to you, who should serenely remain in the Youth Group,

Karl Rahner

TWENTY-TWO

THE DISHONEST CHRISTIAN?

Dear Father Rahner:

I would like to write you about a discord that dwells in my actually very happy life and I would be glad to receive some advice from you. We Christians have a very beautiful motto for our life: "Love thy neighbor as thyself." And we—myself included—initiate and engage in activities in our life with this lofty aim in view. For example, I sometimes work in a hospital for handicapped children, or I write birthday cards to elderly people, some of whom are relatives. I try, to a certain extent, to be nice and friendly with my fellow human beings. Sometimes, however, my mother says to me: "You do a lot of talking about love of neighbor, but you don't hesitate to criticize me if I wrangle with those around me. But you actually do nothing concrete in that sense, nor have you yet to assume any kind of responsibility (of course!), and within the family you tend to forget your high-sounding words." When I reflect on it, she is quite right. For, on the one hand, I do talk a lot about how one could live life according to Jesus' conception, and on the other, I am very indolent when it's a question of attending to my aunt or to any kind of unpleasant task.

I believe that the problem lies in the fact that I always associate love of neighbor with a grandiose deed of which I am the center as much as possible. And this deed must then rise above the routine of every day. Conversely, however, the normal, pleasant family life could also signify love of others. Or when as, for example, I have just done, I break off with a friend I will simply have nothing more to do with him or her, I react condescendingly and spitefully, I am cynical and probably cut a ridiculous figure. But I fancy myself as somehow superior when I make him or her sense my aversion. But then what should I do? I know that the commandment to love one's neighbor would enjoin me to behave quite normally in all respects despite the end of the friendship. Yet I simply can't get myself to act accordingly.

Perhaps this point clearly shows how difficult it really is for me to be a Christian. Seemingly, it is easy for me to be outwardly good, but in a small, private circle I don't have the courage and strength to initiate a move towards reconciliation and forgiveness. I would gladly be an honest Christian, but I can make no progress.

Dear Father Rahner, could you help me to extricate myself from this knotty discord?

With many kind regards,

Renata

Dear Renata,

Your mother, at bottom, is right, although her reproach can actually be directed against all persons and presumably also against herself. We talk lots about love of neighbor (at least when we ourselves do not want to practice it, but expect it from others).

These words remain just words, high-sounding to be sure, but we never really actualize them in concrete life, in the family, in our surroundings and in connection with the tasks of everyday life. It can nevertheless be quite meaningful if you do break off a friendship from which nothing positive can accrue. But this need not be a violation of the commandment to love one's neighbor. It goes without saying that you should never be condescending, spiteful and cynical on separating from a former friend. That would really be a violation of the injunction to love your neighbor, a love that you still owe him or her.

You say that you cannot make progress in regard to this commandment, even though you would like to be an honest Christian. We all find ourselves in this situation at one time or another, in that we fall short of this moral categorical imperative. This knotty discord certainly exists. It is difficult to extricate oneself from it. Nor do I have a simple recipe on how to effect such a triumphal observance of the commandment. All we can do is patiently and repeatedly take upon ourselves the tasks that our fellow humans set before us and try to cope with them—with their cares, their demands, including those that get on our nerves. You cannot instantly actualize *ideal* love of neighbor, but you can now in the course of the daily routine accept the neighbor, the other who happens to cross your path, by being gracious, helpful and tolerant. Do that and then your whole life itself will be an extrication from the knotty discord from which you are suffering.

Cordially,

Karl Rahner

TWENTY-THREE

CAN ONE ALWAYS REMAIN A CHILD?

Dear Father Rahner,

I am a person who is particularly sensitive with regard to the reactions of those in my milieu, even though sometimes I refuse to take notice of them. But there are times when I become particularly aware of the suffering of an individual, indeed the suffering of all humankind. For I can become infinitely sad when I reflect on how many are the moments of disappointment that mark a life time, how many unfulfilled longings, how many unnecessary vexations. At the same time, big and small events come to mind which, in an absolute long-range sense, weigh heavily on me in different ways and with a continuing effect, but in the immediate moment occasion the same distress, the same tears, the same pain.

Most times I am thinking naturally of situations in which I myself am subject to extreme emotional fluctuations, hence of moments when I am very happy or very sad. But I note that I myself am not strengthened and am not better prepared for "adulthood" through the many "pin-pricks," the minor and major difficulties that crop up in my sunny and happy life. On the contrary—I have the feeling that a particle of me is repeatedly being lost, being shattered and painfully separated from me, the child that I in full honesty want to be before God and life.

I pose the philosophical question that asks whether this kind of preparation for life is in itself necessary and meaningful for a human being, whether in times of need he or she does not receive the needed strength as a gift from God. In other words, whether humans need to exert themselves or be trained beforehand in order to muster up this strength. And I also pose the theological question that, out of the deepest conviction, asks whether one may trust that God is actually a loving and helpful father. I must altogether personally and without presumption and exaggeration say that I have repeatedly experienced how God as father protects me, precisely when I am positively stymied by a cluster of confused feelings or exposed to an extremely stressful situation. And it is then that God helps me by showing me a way, a ray of hope, and all I must do is to muster up the courage to venture onward.

I am often reproached for being a weakling because I am too credulous, too sentimental, too emotional and compassionate. But after all the experiences that were granted to me, I simply believe that in my life I must seek the good and that I am bound to do this good, that I must not be as realistic and as "grown up" as possible, but that I can remain a child. That furthermore I, as a lay person, despite all failures or insufficient or futile efforts, should talk of the divine and should profess Christianity as the most important aim in life.

I would gladly like to believe all this but I feel alone, abandoned and plunged in doubt, particularly when I see other persons assume an air of condescending superiority vis-a-vis my utterances, persons who I thought still shared with me our ideals of childhood. I then feel very insecure and seemingly overcome by such superior doubters.

Probably many live in this loneliness of decision, many are disheartened by the mite of suffering in the seemingly so sunny everyday life, many have unlearned the bright laughter of the child. But is there not a comfort, a hope, also with values which are just as valid in this world as the many other values which since our childhood we have been raised to view and accept as eminently proper and worth striving for?

Dear Father Rahner, I would really be very thankful to you if you would show me a way in my (childish) insecurity in this area that would lead me further forward and give me sureness in my faith. And that would also lead me out of the well of my inner loneliness.

I thank you in advance.

Irene

Dear Irene,

If I wanted to be honest, I could first of all say that your letter is a typical letter of one who is in the transitional period that marks the passage from the phase of childhood to adulthood. The letter is clever, almost somewhat contrivedly so. It poses a philosophical question which comes from the heart rather than from direct experiences of concrete life. I shall not address myself at all to this aspect of your letter.

I admire you rather because of your capacity to selflessly interest yourself in others and in their sorrows and disappointments. Perhaps this is an inclina-

tion which is not yet necessarily a Christian virtue that
is born of a selfless freedom. But such a predisposi-
tion can really be the point of departure for really
becoming a human being who, in freedom, is selflessly there for others. Such starting points are always a
great task that God sets before us. Given your bent to
be there for others, you should not let yourself
become unsure because of the reaction of the people
of your milieu who selfishly think only of themselves.
You should serenely guard against becoming too
''realistic'' and ''grown-up.'' Such realistic
adulthood, after all, is often only unfettered egoism,
which lets the true life of a human being wither. For
the true human being, as he or she really should be,
must have the courage to acknowledge and proclaim
the great and happiness-making experiences of his or
her life and preserve them, the experience that God's
fatherly love protects, that new roads open up
repeatedly in life along which one can progress further if one but musters up the courage to see these
paths.

Don't let yourself be driven into a state of doubt
and driven to unsureness by people conceited by their
assertedly superior scepticism. If they continue along
this line, such people, over the long run, will stiffen in
sterility. They then become petty, pathetic philistines.
Such persons want to be cunning and avoid suffering
and disappointments. They dismiss all great and deep
feelings as sentimentality to which they feel superior.
But, over the long run, they will become inhuman,
stunted petty bourgeois. Don't be impressed or in-
fluenced by them! Have the courage to risk something
and here and there even to become disappointed with
yourself, with others and with exterior life. That is of
no real consequence. It is better that on occasion

one's feelings be a bit confused rather than that one resign oneself to the idea that one should no longer dare to have any.

Adulthood and genuine childlikeness are not mutually exclusive contradictions. And if you, up to now, have been and are a happy person in the different dimensions of your life, then you should, in a grateful acknowledgment of what God had granted you, not let yourself be rendered unsure by a modern scepticism, by persons of our day who assert that disappointment alone is the truth.

I have heard that you are an excellent assistant in the youth group and that you are also successful in your studies. When someone serenely, and with thankfulness to God, accepts such a life and, at the same time, also is ever prepared to go forward along the right path, even when he or she is passing through difficult times, he or she must accept the cheerfulness and the felicity in his or her life with childlike unaffectedness and by so doing indeed becomes a real adult.

With all best wishes.

Karl Rahner

TWENTY-FOUR

I CAN'T BE ALONE

Dear Father Rahner,

I don't know whether you can still remember the girl dressed in white who presented you with the gift at the birthday celebration of our group. I was the girl. About a week ago when I visited the pastoral director of our youth group we discussed some very serious problems for which I simply had no solution. He was of the opinion that I could confidently turn to you for counsei since they were all matters that concerned many young people.

So I am permitting myself to tell you something about myself and my questions. I am 20 years old, I am studying theology and would like to be a pastoral assistant. I have been away from my family for about a year and am living in a small room of my own. In the beginning I greatly enjoyed this freedom, but now it is becoming something of a problem for me. I have many friends of whom I am very fond and who are also fond of me. Most of them still live with their parents and therefore come here to visit me. In the last months the situation so deteriorated that many people showed up here every night and something was always going on.

I am very happy that these people trust me so that they know that they are always welcome (and really so) by me. But I have simply unlearned how to be alone and actually also unlearned how to have stillness around me so that I can pray properly. I have become very restless and nervous, my relationships go into greater disorder daily, I sleep too little and there is much more else to tell.

On the other hand, I simply cannot endure it when for once no one shows up and nothing is going on. What's more, I am unable to send someone packing and to tell him or her that I would like to be alone sometime. There are indeed often people whom I know are lonesome, who need help, need me.

It's very difficult for me to find a solution because I also note how very much I myself need people, how I can't get along without them, even though over the long run it wears me out.

I would like really once more to enjoy stillness, to be able to pray again, only I don't find the right way because I don't want to lose my friends and also because I would honestly like to help people.

I wanted simply to relate all this to you and I would be very happy to receive a few lines from you.

Cordial greetings.

Maria

Dear Maria,

I most surely remember you from the birthday celebration.

Strictly speaking and perhaps somewhat reduced to its ultimate essence, your problem is the problem of authentic human freedom. Just imagine if freedom, where it is genuine and alive, consisted merely in doing one thing and simply dropping the other, then it would be relatively easily and neatly constituted in human life. Naturally there are certain situations as regards human freedom in which a clear, hard decision for or against something must be taken. One cannot marry two persons at once. Under certain circumstances—for example for persons like myself—one obviously gives up smoking if there's the danger of succumbing to the vice of nicotine addiction. If one becomes a Carthusian, he to a certain extent radically closes the door to much of what ordinarily crops up in the life of other humans.

In short, there are many decisions made on the basis of freedom that simply signifies a flat, hundred percent yes or no. But very often things proceed differently, and the other situation of freedom must indeed be perceived, accepted and endured.

In other words very often a person is not only in practice prevented but also prohibited from making such simple, hundred percent decisions. A monk, for example, decides to be poor through a vow. Despite that, however, he has a warm room, clean linen and perhaps receives a better lunch than many others who are poor in a much more bitter way than he. That is not only the way things stand but also as they ought to be and must be.

Expressed more generally: life is mostly an unavoidable mixture of contrary realities. You perhaps sometimes sit in a stillness-suffused church, then you may go to a dance where many people whirl about confusedly amid lots of noise. At another time you take a walk by yourself, another time someone is with you whose presence gladdens and comforts you. We must realize that in many circumstances of our life, we cannot, and also should not, renounce such a remarkable mixture of which our life is compounded.

Nevertheless, there is in all this a real problem which is also yours. It would be easy if you went to a Carmelite cloister and gave up all your former friends. It would be easy, if you wanted simply to lose yourself in the unguided and irresponsible hustle and bustle of your life. But you may do neither the one or the other. Rather you must, to an extent that this is possible, effect a reasonable mixture (if I may put it so) of the contradictory things in your life. That certainly is very hard to do.

There are, for example, people (I'm not one of them) who quite sensibly say that they now and then allow themselves a cigarette for their relaxation and enjoyment but who despite this do not become chain-smokers. Such a lifestyle—although not applicable and recommendable to everybody—is altogether a sensible way of enjoyment. Thus there are also in your life, as you yourself note, opposites to be united and rightly configured. To this also belongs the capacity now and then decisively to renounce something and yet, at the same time, not easily transform this renunciation into a one-sided radicalism. Therein, I think, lies your problem.

You must find the courage and the resolve really to study, and also to be able to be alone. And not let yourself be constantly followed around by friends and acquaintances and under certain circumstances you must energetically show them the door when you have something important to do. But you should also not want to cheapen life by living like a hermit. See to it, with a certain responsible energy, that you get the sleep you require, prescribe in advance certain rules for the conduct of your life to which you must strictly adhere, checking on your performance accordingly.

St. Ignatius of Loyola (upon discovering such rules of conduct for himself) also hinted that one should, to a certain extent, try to find the rules for one situation in the other situation. When one is roaringly hungry one should not ask how much he or she should reasonably eat. This question should be posed where one is not especially hungry. If one caught up in life's crush and hustle and bustle longs for solitude, the situation perhaps exists for one to ask oneself how he or she could gain by fighting such a desire for solitude and stillness. This guided, planned mixture in the life that one should lead is a task that must always be mastered anew, and one more difficult to live than an inflexible, fanatically lived way of life.

You should not want to give up your friends and you should not become a person who can no longer be still and pray. I cannot give you a recipe for making this mixture in your life. You yourself must find this so-called dialectical life style. One must be able to improvise and, at the same time, give oneself certain norms to which one adheres. Try an exercise some time in which you step out of your normal life of solitude and busyness so that you can soberly, self-critically test both ingredients of your life before God. By doing so you will better perceive how this mixture of your life, which is your task, can really be found on your own.

If you now live alone, you are now more responsible for yourself than previously was the case. And your dwelling, to a certain extent, is the testing ground for a responsible life-style in which amid all the experiences and even the contrarieties, the task is to find an ultimate and responsible harmony.

With cordial greetings,

Karl Rahner